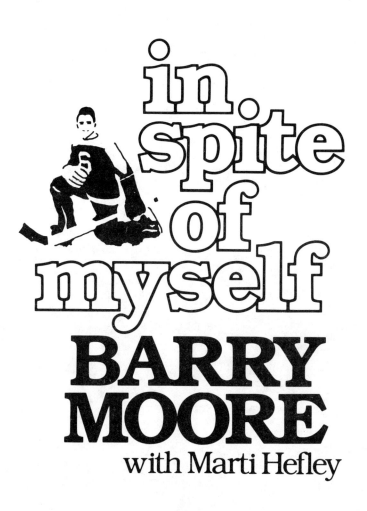

in spite of myself

BARRY MOORE

with Marti Hefley

Tyndale House
Publishers, Inc.
Wheaton, Illinois

First printing, May 1982

Library of Congress Catalog Card Number 82-80374
ISBN 0-8423-1581-0, paper
Copyright © 1982 by James Hefley, Marti Hefley,
and Crusade Evangelism International.
All rights reserved.

Printed in the United States of America

To Butch

CONTENTS

ONE
PLAYING TO WIN

I might as well tell you right up front, this is more than just the story of my life. It's an illustration of how God works in the lives of those who seek to serve him. It has some laughs, and a few tears, and at times it may be brutally frank. All the questions are not answered. Sometimes I have realized *later* why God allowed certain events to occur in my life; and there are other things I still don't understand. But I know this: God in his sovereignty and grace has laid his hand upon my life. Beyond my wildest expectations, he has opened doors of opportunity. Often his power has been demonstrated through me, not because I am special or unique, but in spite of myself!

A review of the past years is awe inspiring to me. More important than the statistics are the testimonies of transformed lives. In recent years it seems that wherever I go I meet someone who tells me, "I received Christ in one of your crusades." Or, "I've spent the past ten years on the mission field, because of a decision made when I heard you speak years ago." Now, that has to be God's doing, because I surely couldn't have pulled it off by myself.

Reports like those often make me think back to the greatest spiritual confrontation in my own life. I was eighteen years old, and a recent high school graduate. One day some of the men from our church, Wortley Road Baptist, came and talked to me about being baptized. I had been raised in the church and I guess I showed enough religious savvy to convince them that I was really a Christian, but I had not been baptized and therefore was not a member of the church.

I knew that Christ had died for my sins and all the rest, but I still wanted to have some fun in my life. I thought of Bible-toting young people as "Holy Joes" who were living a boring existence. I was willing to be baptized, but I was not going to give up dancing and movies. I got the impression that the church was willing to accept me on my terms, so I agreed to be immersed the following Sunday night with a couple of my contemporaries.

I walked down the steps into the water that night basically worrying that I might get water up my nose, cough and sputter, and make a fool of myself.

The pastor intoned some solemn words about how this act signified I was identifying myself with Jesus Christ. The congregation began singing as I was lowered into the water, and I came back up hearing the words, "*Free from the law, O happy condition.*" I climbed out carefully, for the steps were a bit slippery. "*Jesus hath bled, and there is remission.*" I hesitated just a moment at the top of the landing, then exited from the sanctuary down a short flight of steps into a large Sunday school assembly room. "*Cursed by the law and bruised by the fall, Grace hath redeemed us once for all.*"

The room was empty. I had expected one of the deacons to meet me with a towel, but I guess they were busy with the others. "*Once for all, O sinner, receive it, Once for all, O brother, believe it.*" There was a large tray on the floor, which I stepped into so I wouldn't get water all over the place. "*Cling to the cross, the burden will fall, Christ hath redeemed us once for all.*"

I was standing there dripping, all by myself with those words swirling around in my brain, when I heard a voice. It couldn't have been more real if it were audible. The words sent a chill up my spine, "Barry, did you really mean it?" I forgot to breathe. Had I really meant it? Or was this the most sacrilegious act of my life?

10

The challenge stung. Was I really willing to live for Christ, or was I just another phony? Instinctively I threw up a fist in a gesture more associated with a sporting event than with church, and I prayed, "Dear God, I'll give it a go, if you'll go with me!" And I meant it.

I was still a little shaken as I toweled off and changed clothes, for I hadn't expected this to be a life-changing experience. Yet I had given my word, and for me that was a total commitment. It couldn't be just a half-hearted experiment.

My mind whirled to my past. What had brought me to this decision? I'd gone to church all my life. As a matter of fact, one of my earliest memories was of Dad pulling me to church on a white sleigh. With soft flakes drifting down through a dim London, Ontario, winter morning, he would trudge through the squeaky cold snow the mile and a half from our chocolate brown, two-story stucco house on Langarth Street to what seemed to me a towering edifice on Wortley Road.

He used to stand the sleigh against the side of the church building and we'd climb the stairs to the sanctuary with its glorious stained glass windows. Sitting next to him I'd feel safe and content, and somewhat proud. He was Edwin Wilbur Moore and I was Edwin Barry. Although I'd always been called Barry, I liked sharing my father's name, and I would be pleased when someone would say, "My, but you look just like your daddy."

After church we would return to our warm house that would be filled with the tantalizing smells of our waiting dinner. My mother, Erma Dear Moore, couldn't attend church while my sister Kathy was a baby, since there was no nursery then. After dinner we would listen to the radio preachers until time for afternoon Sunday school. James McGinley was one of their favorites, and I used to enjoy the sound of the rich Scottish brogue of the fiery Baptist pulpiteer long before I was old enough to understand his message.

We'd return home after Sunday school, have a light meal, and be back in church for the evening services. The whole day was spent going to and from church. I'd always been

11

taught that Sunday was the Lord's day. I'd known about Jesus for as long as I could remember, but when had he become real to me?

Not long after I'd put my five pennies in the lighthouse-shaped birthday bank in the Sunday school, there had been a special children's meeting that had made a deep impression on me. C. J. Loney, an elderly Baptist pastor from Hamilton, came to lead it. He wore a long ministerial coat with wing-tipped collared shirts and a bow tie and seemed to have a special flair with children.

"Where's my song leader?" he had begun. "I need someone to lead the choruses, and I'll pay a nickel to whomever will do it." The kids had all giggled and squirmed and looked at each other, but I thought, "Boy, a whole nickel!" because in those days that was a lot of money. So with suspicious motivation, I volunteered to "serve the Lord" by leading singing.

The thing that really stood out in my mind, though, was the white flag he had had on the platform to represent the "Army of the Lord." At the end of the service Mr. Loney called for all those who wanted to enlist in God's army to go and stand near that flag. One by one, about 125 or 130 kids got up and walked over to the flag while I just stood there with my heart pounding. It was a tremendously emotional experience for me, for I had the feeling that I might be left. I wasn't worried about anyone laughing at me or anything like that, I just didn't want to be left out of the Lord's army. Finally, when the service was just about to close, I, too, stepped out and with great sincerity made a public declaration that I was on God's side.

That experience hadn't made a profoundly dramatic change in my young life. I was only a child, so my life went on as usual.

Another time, when I was eleven, I had expressed a desire to be God's child. My mother took me with her to hear Charles Templeton down at the old London Gospel Tabernacle one Friday night. The illustrious cartoonist-journalist had recently been converted and was to give his testimony.

I was mesmerized by the handsome, articulate, brilliant speaker. His recounting of his experience with God made me long for such an exciting encounter. When the invitation was given at the end of the service, I raised my hand, indicating I wanted to be a Christian. The singing continued, but I made no move to go to the front of the huge auditorium. A lady sitting behind us leaned over and asked if I wanted to publicly respond. "I'll go with you," she offered kindly. I shook my head. I was too timorous to walk to the front, even at the urging of such a golden-throated orator.

Later, riding home on the streetcar, my mother and I talked over how one became a Christian, and what it meant to accept the Lord into your heart. She had seemed satisfied that I understood, and for a time it seemed there was a change in my life, but when I reached high school and temptations came my way, it seemed so easy to opt for fun rather than being concerned with serving the Lord.

That indifferent attitude had continued until my baptismal experience tonight. Somehow I knew that the commitment I had made in the assembly room was going to change my life. I finished changing my clothes, combed my hair until it was just so, and then left the church to walk to my girl friend's house. I normally moved along at a fast clip, but tonight I sauntered along as I wondered what I should tell Helen. She was a very nice girl, and quite attractive, but she had made no secret of the fact that she was a little leery of people who were "holier than thou."

I trudged up the steps to Helen's house, and her mother let me in. Helen was sitting in the living room on the corner sofa. A lamp behind her was lighting the open book on her lap, and at the same time was setting off highlights in her soft blonde hair. The deep blue dress she was wearing made her eyes look even bluer than usual as she gazed up at me expectantly. She had never seemed more appealing.

Hesitantly, I sat down beside her. She was an exceptionally pleasant, feminine girl and I enjoyed being with her. We'd had a lot of fun together the past two or three months, and I didn't want to do or say anything that would bring our relationship to an end, but I knew I had to tell her about the decision I had just made.

"I, um, was baptized tonight, you know?"

"Yes, you told me you were going to be."

"Well, you know my church teaches that a Christian shouldn't go dancing or to shows and I, well, I just can't go to some of the places we've been going lately. But there are lots of other places we could go, and fun things to do. So you won't mind, will you?"

I'd blurted the whole paragraph out in one gulp, and then took a deep breath, waiting for her reply. I caught a faint whiff of her perfume. She smiled sweetly, and I thought I was going to melt.

"Barry, I respect your stand, but I'm not going your way," she replied in a definite tone.

There was no basis for arbitration, so I started home with the feeling of lead in my stomach and mush in my shoes.

"Big fat deal!" I thought. "I surrender to the Lord, and the first thing he does is take away my girl!" I wondered how the other people in my life would react.

My folks would probably be pleased. But my sister Kathy? I wasn't sure. Kathy had always been a kind of ideal younger sister—she went her way, and I went mine. Even as a little kid she had always been a girly-girl who preferred to sit at home having tea parties with her friend Enid Carter while I was out playing rough-and-tumble games with the older boys.

Kathy's platinum hair, blue eyes, and fair coloring had always been attention-getters, since Mother, Father, and I were all dark. I remembered how Mother would patiently explain that our maternal grandmother was also very fair, while Kathy smiled and batted her big blues, glorying in all the attention. At sixteen, she was now a real scene stealer, and I was sometimes suspicious about whether my friends were coming to visit me or to get a chance to be with her.

All in all there had been little sibling rivalry between us. Kathy was always helping Mother in the kitchen, and I'd shovel coal into the monstrous old furnace in our basement, or haul in ice for the ice box, as the season dictated. I didn't really expect her to hassle me or tease me about my decision.

14

"What about the guys at The Booth?" I thought. Now that was another matter.

The Booth was the hangout for the young guys in our neighborhood. It was just a block and a half away at the corner of Briscoe and Cathcart, and had been the hub of my world. The little hole-in-the-wall place had two booths, a table, a pinball machine, and a record player that ground out the tunes of Duke Ellington, Glenn Miller, Benny Goodman, and other Big Bands.

Al Brazier, the proprietor, was a good guy. He was about thirty, and had a gimpy leg from a childhood bout with polio. He'd sell us candy bars and Pepsis, magazines and smokes, and let us hang around and shoot the breeze, play cards, tell dirty stories, and predict the fate of current sports events.

I'd started frequenting the establishment when I entered grade nine at South Collegiate. Because I was still four years old when I started kindergarten, and later skipped grade four, I was younger than the other fellows. I guess I was accepted because I had proven I could keep up with them in most sports.

It was really neat to be able to call out, "Hey, Mom, I'm going over to The Booth," and know there would be someone there to play a game of Euchre or gin rummy. The big thing was to buy a Pepsi and a pack of Gilchrist butter tarts. For the price of one dime I'd feel as if I were sitting on top of the world. Fitting in. Being one of the guys.

When Canada entered World War II my friends began enlisting, but I was much too young. One of the first to go was Alex Woodcock, a friendly, outgoing guy who was extremely well liked. When he came home on furlough and visited The Booth in his Navy uniform, the place exploded. We were all fascinated by his exploits and listened with rapt attention. His life seemed so glamorous that a number of the other guys joined the Navy, too.

Conscription began and the Army called in its share, but many of the boys had already volunteered.

Then word came that Alex's ship, a Corvette, had been sunk by a submarine in the Atlantic. A somber bunch of guys sat around The Booth discussing that event.

"He couldn't be dead," one after another of them opined, with shaking head.

"Naw, he must be out there holding onto some driftwood some place. They'll find him for sure," was the consensus.

But they didn't.

Then it was Bobby Loft. He was a nice little guy I used to go to hockey games with. I remember seeing him looking so sharp in his Air Force grays, but his plane was shot down, and I never saw him again.

It got to be a daily ritual to check the lists in the afternoon paper, looking for names of friends or relatives. There was such a feeling of loss when the name of a buddy or neighbor would appear. It was a sobering experience, yet it seemed to draw those of us who were left closer to each other. It made us more aware of how precious life is.

Because the guys at The Booth were so important to me, I had to wonder if they would comprehend the stand I had just taken for Christ.

I recalled that Gordie Tapp used to play his harmonica and guitar at Briscoe Baptist Church, and none of the guys ever teased him about that. He and his sister, Bernice, even sang duets before he joined the military. He had entered some talent contest in the Army, did the same old jokes and impersonations that used to regale us in The Booth, and had won. He was now serving as master of ceremonies for the Canadian Army Show, which was a big deal, and all the fellows were proud of him.

"Naw," I concluded, "they won't give me too much of a hard time. I just hope my life isn't too boring."

I turned into the canopied street that was my home turf. As a little shaver I had lived at 194 Langarth. Then my parents had bought our house at 193 which was right next to my grandfather's home at 191. With my Uncle Roll and Aunt Willa right across the street at 190, this corner of the world seemed very much to belong to the Moores.

I went in the side door of our house and snuck up the stairs so I wouldn't wake anyone. As I lay wide-eyed on my bed at the front of the house, I wondered just what was going to become of my life. My days were well ordered for the next few weeks because I was obligated to finish my Farm Service.

The Farm Service had seemed like a good deal the minute I heard of it. It seemed that with so many men away fighting the war, there was a need for manpower on the farms. To provide this, young men who were still in high school could agree to work on a farm from Easter through summer, letting grades at Eastertime be considered final marks. It was perfect. Instead of sitting in class, I could be earning seventeen dollars a week, while improving my physical condition. I'd be doing my patriotic duty and I wouldn't have to sweat my final exam in Latin. So I had learned to drive a tractor, had shoveled compost, dug ditches, picked radishes and carrots and cabbages, and whatever. It had turned out to be harder work than I had imagined, but I rather enjoyed it, and I was still eligible to pitch for the South Maroons, our school baseball team.

Well, my days would be full. There was a young people's meeting at the church on Monday night, prayer meeting on Wednesday night, a ball game on Friday, but where could I take a date on Saturday if we didn't go to a dance or a movie? Matter of fact, who would I take anyway now that Helen and I had had a parting of our ways? "God, you are really going to have to help me," I sighed as I rolled over and went to sleep.

At the young people's meeting the next night I watched while a woman I knew led the singing. Traditionally, they would have a man as song leader, but with so many of them away in the service, it was left for whoever could do it to take over. "I could do that," I thought. Standing up there, announcing the page numbers, and waving your arms didn't look like much of a trick. Besides, I had had experience—I'd done it once for Mr. Loney when I was five.

While the speaker for the evening was droning on, I contemplated volunteering. Leading singing for forty or fifty people in the assembly room of Wortley Church didn't seem like a very auspicious way to launch a life of service for Christ, but I couldn't think of anything else I could do. "It would be better than doing nothing," I decided. "At least this time I won't be doing it to get a nickel."

I told the leader after the meeting broke up, "If you'd like, I could lead the singing for young people's sometimes."

She blinked a couple of times and raised her eyebrows. I hadn't been the most faithful attender at the meetings. I would come only if I had nothing more interesting going, so it was understandable that she would be surprised at my display of interest.

"Sure, Barry, that would be great," she replied at last. "You can take over next week."

I figured I'd get Harry McKenzie to give me a few pointers, since I couldn't admit that I didn't know what I was doing. Harry was about ten or fifteen years older than I was, and a faithful worker in the church. He had attended London Bible Institute and had gotten instruction in songleading there, so I asked him for a crash course.

Harry took me into one of the Sunday school rooms off the main assembly room and taught me the patterns for 3/4 and 4/4 songs. He gave me a couple of hints about how to get people singing enthusiastically, and then it was "Watch out young people, here I come."

I got up there the next Monday night and pretended I knew what I was doing, and no one seemed to catch on that I was bluffing my way through it. If anyone had requested a song in 6/8 it would have blown my cover completely, but what I lacked in knowledge I covered over with what probably appeared to be a cocky attitude.

Getting involved that way made Monday nights more fun, and I filled in the blanks on my social calendar with sports. I guess I should explain that early in my childhood I had fallen in love with anything round that I could hit, kick, throw, or bounce. My mother always delighted in telling people how my father would play catch with me while I was still a toddler.

Besides playing in any kind of a game going, I enjoyed being transported via the magic of the ether waves to Tiger Stadium in Detroit, where I could experience the thrill of a double play executed by the incomparable combination of "Rogell to Gehringer to Greenberg." The sweet sound of ol' Hank getting good wood on a ball and knocking it out of the park would send me into ecstasy. A shut out by School-boy Rowe would keep me glued to the set more than any mystery thriller.

During hockey season my loyalties were with the Toronto Maple Leafs. My heros were Gordie Drillon, Walter "Turk" Broda, and Syl Apps. Besides listening to every game aired, I cut pictures of all the sports greats from the newspapers and arranged them in scrapbooks.

The first team I had an opportunity to play with was the Kensington Park Tecumsehs in the Pee Wee league. As leadoff batter I experienced the thrill of victory when we won the championship and were presented crests as mementos of our fabulous season. From then on my summers were devoted to baseball. Perhaps the biggest thrill was the game that produced a banner on the sports page proclaiming "BARRY MOORE HURLS NO-HIT, NO-RUN JUNIOR WIN."

My involvement in sports had taught me a few principles— such as, being willing to sacrifice other pleasures to work on your primary goal; being willing to work at perfecting the skill chosen as most important; learning the rules, and abiding by them; and giving it all you've got.

I had had some disadvantages when I entered team sports. I was small for my age and younger than most of my classmates, but I had some things going for me, too. I had good coordination and I was quick. I had also become fast, because I'd often had to outrun some bigger guy to save my own skin. I had an amazing amount of natural energy to channel into the sport of the season. Perhaps most important, I was willing to give it my all. Surely some of these same principles could be applied to living for Christ.

Leading singing didn't bring the cheering crowds or the thrill of victory, but I determined to put as much energy into that as I did into sports. If I could just find a half-decent-looking girl, who had a dedication to Christ, I'd be content. After all, I had been quarterback of our high school football team, and was used to getting attention from the coeds. The idea of not having a date for Saturday night really hurt my pride, but I couldn't be content with some religious square who looked like Olive Oyle with orthopedic shoes and a bun in her hair.

I was sitting in my usual pew at the back of the church where I could lean my head against the wall and drape my arm over the end of the pew, brooding over my dilemma a couple of Sundays later, while waiting for the services to begin. The choir door wiggled in the characteristic manner that indicated the procession was about to begin. First out the door was a petite brunette with doe-like eyes. Audrey. Audrey Snelgrove. Hmmmmmmmm.

TWO
A GIRL NAMED BUTCH

I'd never really been introduced to the Snelgroves, but I knew who they were. The family had been attending Wortley Church the past year since Mr. Snelgrove's conversion and baptism. He had the pleasant disposition that all barbers should have, and always had a smile for everyone. His wife taught a class of little kids in Sunday school and seemed to be a perfect complement to her friendly husband.

I knew Audrey was about the right age for me, since she was in Kathy's Sunday school class. There was a little brother, Graham, running around, but he was only fourteen or fifteen, so I hadn't paid much attention to him.

"Should I get someone to introduce me to Audrey?" I wondered. That seemed rather silly, since my family was a fixture in the church and I was certain everyone knew who we were. I finally decided, "nothing ventured, nothing gained," and after my class let out that afternoon I made my way down to the Beginners' Department where Audrey was helping her mother with her Sunday school class.

I knocked on the pale green door and Mrs. Snelgrove answered.

"Is Audrey here?"

"Why, yes, she is," she answered with a question in her voice.

Audrey came to the door and smiled up at me. Now when

21

you're only 5'8" it's always nice to find a girl you can tower over.

"Hi," I said in my most carefree, debonair manner, "I was wondering if you are going to be busy right after church this evening. Would you care to go for a little walk?"

She kind of half turned away from me, then looked over her shoulder with those soft brown eyes and smiled. "All right," she agreed with a gentle sigh.

As we headed up Wortley Road toward Dundas Street that evening, we had opportunity to get to know each other better.

"Have you always lived in London?" I asked.

"No, we moved from a little village named Mt. Brydges when I was eight. I started attending Wortley Church shortly after that."

"Oh? I guess I never noticed you much, until your dad started coming."

"People often don't notice me," she giggled at herself nervously. "I guess I'm too quiet."

"Oh, I don't know about that." She seemed sweet and shy to me. Rather appealing. "I've lived here all my life. On Langarth Street except for a couple of years we lived on Blackfriars Street."

"Oh?"

"Yeah, my Grandmother Dear died shortly after I finished grade six, so my folks rented our house out for a couple of years and we went to stay with my grandfather. It wasn't bad; he's really quite an interesting character. I tell you, Billy Dear could be right out of a Charles Dickens novel. He's of English descent, although he was born in Kingston, Ontario, and is quite Canadian. He has a habit of calling me 'Barrymore,' as if my name were one word. I can hear him now calling, 'Barrymore, get out of that hen house!'

"He would often punctuate his commands with a squirt of chewing tobacco. He used to sit about two feet in front of the coal stove in the kitchen, with his glasses sliding down the end of his nose, reading the newspaper. From time to time he'd spit out of the side of his mouth at the pan of ashes in front of the old range. Boy, when he missed! What a mess!" I laughed, remembering the familiar scene, and

22

Audrey laughed with me. She seemed so interested in my tale that I continued rattling on.

"Another great thing about living over there was I got to go to Kensington Park, and that's where I really got into baseball. I had some excellent coaching, and got to be a pretty good pitcher. I'm still playing for the South Collegiate team. You'll have to come and see me pitch some time."

I took her smile as an affirmative answer, and held the door of Master's Restaurant open for her. After we settled into a booth and ordered a couple of butterscotch sundaes, I continued my monologue.

"We were still living on Blackfriars when the big flood came in the spring of '37."

"Oh!" Her rounded eyes and raised eyebrows indicated that she knew it had been London West that was hit so hard.

"Yeah, I'll never forget that experience. It rained and rained and the water was so high that people were worried about it coming over the banks of the Thames. The next afternoon our school principal, Mr. Fowler, walked in and quietly said, 'Students, I think you had better pack up your books and go home as quickly as you can.'

"The water was already six to eight inches deep along the curbs, so I walked down the middle of the street. The water was gushing so hard it was obvious the river had overflowed its banks. I dashed into our house and headed for my hockey equipment. I dragged it into the attic where I felt it would be safe. Dad got home soon after and we evacuated to mother's Aunt Alice's house where it was high and dry.

"We didn't get back for about two weeks. The water had been 6'6" in the house. You could see the line on the wall where it had stopped. My hockey equipment was safe, but we lost nearly everything else. My dad would go down into the basement with a big coal shovel and scoop up the rotten fruit and canned food that had been stored down there. The furnace was full of mud.

"Upstairs the piano had tipped over, which showed how strong the current had been in there. The radio was ruined;

the stove wouldn't work; all the dishes, bedding, rugs—everything, was covered with mud and slime and smelled like the river bottom.

"My folks had already gone through some tough years and didn't need another tragedy. When I was just a little guy my father went on strike with the International Typographical Union, because he was a linotype operator for *The London Free Press.* That dragged on month after month while Dad tried to find odd jobs as a jackleg carpenter, plumber, mason, whatever. He's very handy and can fix most anything, but jobs and money were scarce during those days.

"Then I'd overhear grownups talking in hushed monotones about the Great Depression. We ate the vegetables my father had grown in our garden and Mother had canned, but as winter wore on it got to the point where Mother would make soup of a bone, celery, carrots, and barley. I can recall having bologna for Sunday dinner, and living on bread and barley soup during the week.

"My father finally got a job with the London Typesetting Company and the family's financial picture improved a bit. Then came the flood. Not much wonder my mother took it so hard. We moved back to our home on Langarth Street after that, and Dad tried to fix up whatever he could. There was no money to replace anything. Guess none of it hurt me, though. I learned the value of a dollar early."

We finished our sundaes and started back toward Audrey's home on Euclid Avenue. That was about a half mile from the church on the uptown side. My house was on the outskirts of town, about two miles from where Audrey lived. It was a pleasant walk since it was a warm spring evening and the company was so enjoyable.

"Would you like to come in for a while?" she asked politely when we reached her home.

"I'd like to, but I'm doing Farm Service, which means I have to take a bus out to the Market Garden at the crack of dawn. What's your schedule this summer?"

"Oh, I work for London Life Insurance Company. I'm a policy checker and I do some typing and filing. I've been there over a year."

"Oh. I have a few more weeks that I'm obligated to work on the farm, and then I don't know what I'll be doing with my life. Wish I did.

"Well, I'll call you."

I whistled all the way home.

When I stopped by to pick her up for young people's the next night she was dressed in a frilly outfit which made her look so dainty and petite and feminine that I said, "Come on, Butch, we're going to be late." I don't think her mother appreciated the nickname, but it was so inappropriate that it stuck. Soon everyone seemed to take it for granted that Butch and Barry were an item.

When it came to a "girl you'd like to take home to Mother," Butch was the ultimate: a sweet, soft-spoken, homey lady. My family took to her right away, and my father even began taking her to see me play baseball. He would patiently explain the rules of the game to her. To make her even more perfect, she was totally infatuated with me, which wasn't bad for the ego.

By this time I had been asked to lead singing for the Sunday school assemblies as well as the young people's meetings, so I guess I wasn't doing too bad a job. The comments I received were all positive and encouraging, so I felt pleased that I had found an outlet for serving my Lord.

Our baseball team, the South Collegiate Maroons, hadn't lost a game, so we made it to the finals of the first all-city tournament. Audrey was in the stands with my dad for the big game, and that made me feel more confident and more nervous at the same time. I was really keyed up for that game! I ran up and down the sidelines trying to work off some of the steam that had built up in me. This was the biggest game I'd ever played in and the 5,000 seats were filled with a wildly partisan, noisy crowd.

"Play ball!"

I scuffed at the pitcher's mound, took a deep breath, went into my windup and threw a fast ball. Whack! A line drive up the middle for a single. That really threw me. I stomped around that mound, stalling, half talking to myself and half praying. "OK, Moore, settle down or you're going to blow it. Lord, help me to do my best. Help me relax and perform the way I've been trained to all these years."

I struck the next two batters out. I pitched the whole game, racking up a total of ten strike outs, and best of all, we won seven to two.

Ah, life was sweet! Until the letter came:

> *Dear Mr. Moore,*
>   *You are requested by the federal government . . .*
> *Canadian armed forces . . . to preserve the peace*
> *and protect our country.*

I was being drafted! Me, a soldier? The glamour of war had long since worn off. If I could just go around and sing to entertain the troops as Gordie Tapp was doing, that would be OK, but the thought of shooting people had almost as much appeal as the idea of being shot at. My mother was all upset, but my father had served in World War I and he just said, "A man's got to do what he's got to do."

I hopped on my bike and rode over to talk to Butch. She looked almost as apprehensive as my mother when I explained the situation. "What are you going to do?" she asked.

"I don't think I have any choice. They've called me up, I'll have to go. I've been wondering what to do when I finished Farm Service, but this wasn't exactly what I had in mind. I don't know what kind of a soldier I'll make. I've never even owned a gun. The only time I ever messed with one I got in trouble."

"Oh?"

"Yeah. Back in first or second year high school a friend of mine, Cuthbert Jones, had a BB gun. We got to messing around with it one day, and I discovered I was a pretty good shot. I noticed a streetlight, and it seemed like the most perfect target in the world. I just had to see if I could hit it. My luck, I got it dead center and destroyed it. I handed Jones the gun and ran for home. About an hour later a motorcycle cop pulled up. Man, was I scared, but he just gave me a warning—which I took to heart. That's my only experience with guns."

"Well, if the Lord doesn't want you to be a soldier, he'll get you out of it somehow," she suggested.

"Yeah. I hope so," I replied unenthusiastically.

I reported as ordered to the Woolsley Barracks, the home of the Royal Canadian Regiment. They put us through the initial induction steps. Gave us our physicals and some psychological and intelligence tests. Ran us through one by one.

When I finished, this big, rough-looking sergeant says to me, "Moore, your M Test isn't bad." I wasn't sure what an "M Test" was, but I was very glad to hear it was OK.

"Matter of fact, it's high enough to qualify you for officer's training college. We think we've got the war in the bag now, though, so we're going to give you a choice. You can either go for officer's training, or you can go home and get some post-high school education, and providing you cut it, you won't have to do military service. But if you blow it, you're in the army."

I suddenly felt the call for a higher education. My grades in high school hadn't been that great, because I'd been more interested in sports than studies, but I would sure crack the books now!

My family seemed relieved, and so did Audrey. "Now I have to make a big decision," I explained to her as she followed me around the Highland Golf Course. Golf was my newest passion and I could hit a ball as if it had been shot from a cannon. If I could only control the direction it took!

"What do your folks say about it?"

"Hmmmm? Oh, the schooling. Well, neither of them went to college, and there's the financing to consider, too. I'm not sure what to do. I've thought about talking to Ken Browne. He's always taken a real interest in the guys in our Sunday school class. As a principal, he's had a better educational background than most people I know, and he's easy to talk to."

"That's a good idea," she agreed.

Sunday night Audrey and I got ourselves invited over to Ken and Kit's house on Raywood Avenue for some homemade ice cream. While lapping mine up, I explained my problem.

"What would you like to do, Barry?" he probed.

"Oh, I'd love to go into professional sports, and I think I could make it in baseball, but I wouldn't play on Sundays, so that eliminates that possibility."

"Have you ever considered teaching?"

"Yes, I have. But I don't know if I'd be much good at it."

"Well, the training you would receive at Normal School would be valuable even if you decided after a while that teaching wasn't for you. Teaching is an opportunity to explore yourself and your relations with others. The same methodological and psychological principles can be applied to other vocations. If the Lord should later lead you into business, you would know much more about establishing relationships and understanding others than someone starting in green. And if you should be called into full-time Christian work, those same basic principles are just as valid in the ministry of the Word as they are in secular areas."

"Sounds as if I couldn't miss."

"Well, you pray about it and we will, too. I realize what an important decision this is for you, Barry."

We talked on until late into the night, and the more we discussed the possibilities, the more content I felt with this decision. I would at least apply to Normal School for the teacher training, and see what happened.

"It'll be easier on the finances, too," I explained to my folks later. "There's no tuition at Normal School, and since it is just a few blocks away, I can walk. I can get a Saturday job to pick up money for books as well as pocket money, and Mr. Browne says since I've had grade thirteen, after I finish Normal School I would have enough credits to get a degree in just two years at the university. I could even teach days and go to university at night and that would make me eligible to be a principal someday."

So that fall I was back in school. For recreation I organized a basketball team and we would play a couple of games a week. I'd call one of the high school Phys. Ed. teachers in town and say, "This is Barry Moore. Have you got a junior team that wants a practice game? We've got six guys over here who can't play, but we'd like to challenge you."

Playing guard gave me an outlet for some of my energy, but I still had one crucial problem to solve. "What do Christians do on Saturday nights?" I asked Butch.

"Well, the Canadian Youth Fellowship has a meeting at the London Labor Temple over the Little Theatre," she suggested.

I gave a shrug and agreed. "Guess so. It has to be better than nothing."

The next Saturday we walked into the small auditorium, and it was packed to the rafters. Most of the guys were in uniform, probably out-of-towners who were stationed nearby. They sang a couple of songs at the top of their voices and then a big, affable guy Butch identified as Ken Welch go up and said, "Barry Moore, will you lead us in prayer?" and he looked straight at me.

I felt the same sick feeling in the pit of my stomach I used to get standing as goalie, waiting for the first puck to come my way in a hockey game. I'd never prayed in public in my life. How did he know my name, anyway?

I stood to my feet as if in a trance. The blood was pounding in my temples, and I could feel sweat starting to break out on my brow. I cleared my throat and tried to think of all the pious phrases I'd heard used all my life. The pressure was greater than pitching with a full count, two out, and the winning run on third. Somehow I managed to come up with what I felt was a passable prayer.

"How'd I do?" I whispered to Butch as I flopped back down beside her.

"All right, I guess," she replied.

"All right," I thought. "All right!" That's all I get? If I'd put forward that much effort on any sports field, the crowd would be cheering its head off. *All right.* I wasn't so sure about this dedicated Christian stuff. I slouched down in my seat and pouted a bit as the speaker made his way to the podium.

A few days later I got a phone call from Ken Welch. "Barry, I'm going to hold a meeting for a group in Woodstock on Thursday night and I need a song leader. Harry McKenzie says you do a good job. How about it?"

Harry? He must have been the one who got Ken to call on

29

me to pray. "Thursday? I don't have anything going on that night. Sure, I'll be glad to help out."

On the ride to Woodstock I discovered that Ken wasn't much older than I was, had graduated from South Collegiate in 1942, and was still studying to become a certified accountant.

"How did you get started working with these youth groups?" I asked.

"We started out having informal meetings for the youth after church on Sunday evenings, and that grew to involve several churches. In 1939 we started operating on Saturday nights on a regular basis and sort of patterned ourselves after a group in Brantford. Our slogan is 'Canada's Youth for Christ.' We give Christian kids a place to go on Saturday nights to find inspiration, fun, and a chance to meet their peers from other churches. We also have an evangelistic outreach among servicemen and teens who might not go to a regular church service."

The more I talked with Welch, the more I admired him. It didn't take much math to figure that if they started in 1939 and he graduated from high school in 1942, he must have been very young. Yet according to Harry, Ken had been the real motivating force behind the movement. I found it exciting to discover that you didn't have to be an old graybeard with a pack of degrees and a Rev. in front of your name before God could use you.

Leading singing that night was fun. The group was very enthusiastic and responded to my feeble attempts at humor as I emceed the program. After that I began going with Ken to various meetings in the area. Sometimes I'd lead singing; sometimes I'd just lead in prayer, but most importantly I began to catch some of the burden for leading young people to Christ. It was exciting to see them step forward at the end of a service to proclaim their faith in him. To think I had had even a small part in that decision brought a thrill greater than any I'd ever gotten in a sports arena.

Then a dilemma presented itself at school. The first months of training had been basically philosophical, and I found that very interesting. I had applied myself, and made good grades. Now they expected me to stand in front of a class and put into practice the principles I'd learned. Was I nervous!

I made out a lesson plan and Butch typed it up for me. It concerned the two parts of a telephone, the receiver and the mouthpiece, and I was going to explain how they worked. I got out to this little white brick country school on Gore Road where they had eight grades in one room. "What are the two main parts of a telephone?" I asked the first question in my well-memorized lesson. A little girl down front seemed to know the answer, so I called on her. "MEtcalf and FAirmount," she responded, giving the names of the two local exchanges. That threw me off, but I managed to bungle through the rest of the lesson.

To my amazement, the kids listened. It was fun. As I got more opportunities to teach, I liked it more and more. I found it amazing that I could really think on my feet, and explain a concept adequately. I loved it. And to think I could get paid for it!

To complete the rosy picture of my life that year, the more time I spent with Butch, the more I realized she was a pretty classy gal. She was so quiet and shy that it took a while to get to know her, but I began to appreciate what a good listener she was. She also had a quick wit and a delightful little half-suppressed giggle that enchanted me. Having her help me with my lesson plans made the work more fun. She made everything more fun.

Yes, that would have been a great year, if I hadn't almost blown up the church.

THREE
THE RULE OF THE RAISED FINGER

When the deacons first approached me about serving as janitor of the church it seemed like a good deal. It would be my responsibility to pick up any refuse lying around, straighten all the hymn books, and make sure the pulpit and the platform were presentable. When the weather got cold, I was to get the fire going early enough to have the building warm when people arrived for the services. And, of course, I'd have to shovel the paths when it snowed.

For this I was to receive the grand sum of seven dollars a week. It didn't sound like much work, and I could certainly use the cash. The biggest inconvenience would be getting there early on Sunday morning and then having nothing to do while waiting for the building to get warm. The solution to that problem was quite simple—the Snelgroves lived just a short way from the church and I figured I could go over and get Mrs. Snelgrove to feed me breakfast. She was quite a cook.

Everything went fine for the first few weeks. Someone had asked me if I knew how to build a fire and I'd chuckled, "Well, sure. You just put paper in, add some wood, and then you build 'er up with coal." I'd done it at home hundreds of times. I used the same technique at the church and everything seemed to work fine. I got a few comments that it wasn't warm enough when services started, but it was fine before they were over. And it stayed warm for the evening events. At the end of the day I pulled all the fire out and banked it. Midweek services were held in the young people's assembly room, which had a separate room heater.

I decided to get there really early the next Sunday and make certain it was warm enough for everyone when they arrived. I went down the concrete floored hall to the furnace room, opened the door to expose the huge old monster of a boiler, and got the kindling going. Then I slid back the paneling across the hall from the doorway which hid the coal bin. I carried shovel after shovel of coal, filling the cavernous furnace with enough fuel to insure the whole building would be heated comfortably. Then I headed to the Snelgroves' for a leisurely breakfast.

About an hour later I returned to check on the temperature. The upstairs was still colder than a bull's horn, so I dashed downstairs to see what the trouble was. I entered the basement assembly room to find water gushing everywhere and the place filled with steam. I dashed toward the boiler, but some of the men were already inspecting it. Then a plumber arrived. I don't know who had called him, but he looked at some gauge and all the color drained from his face. "Great Scott, that thing's about to blow! Get the fire out of there," he yelled, and grabbed a shovel. A number of the men helped him dig the fire out of the furnace and they just dumped it on the concrete floor.

He discovered I had been in charge and turned loose on me. "Look, there's no water over the crown plate!"

"What's a crown plate?" I asked in all innocence.

"Where did you learn to stoke a boiler?"

"Nowhere. They just hired me, and I started to do it."

He took a deep breath and seemed to be trying to compose himself. "You see that gauge?" he asked rhetorically. "When the water gets below that mark, she blows! Another five minutes and your head would have been on the next block! The whole rear end of the church would have been demolished."

By this time the whole congregation was there. Arriving at church to find the building full of steam with water

34

gushing from a ruptured pipe rather upset them. The news that I had almost blown up the building unnerved them even more. What a brouhaha! I decided God had not called me to be a janitor, so I quit. Seven bucks a week wasn't worth it!

Compared to that, the rest of the school year was peaceful. As spring came nearer I became concerned about getting a teaching position. The news from Europe was great, and it looked as if the war would be over before long. But the return of our troops meant they wouldn't be needing many new teachers in the school system. The 115 of us who were graduating were concerned about where we would teach after acquiring all that wisdom over the past year.

I signed up to pitch for the London Majors, a semi-pro team, with the understanding that I wouldn't play on Sundays. As a pitcher I could get away with that because they rotated us. In a town as baseball-conscious as London, this was quite an honor, because some great players came through the ranks of the Majors.

Probably because I was a rookie, some of the guys on the team gave me a hard time about the Sunday thing, but I was determined. There was only one other player who didn't drink, and we were a bit shook up when we discovered on our first road trip that the agenda included "baseball, women, and booze." It was a bit of an education.

My formal education was continuing that summer, for I had signed up for courses at the University of Western Ontario. My finances were still mighty low, but I didn't need much capital. Butch and I walked 'most everywhere we went. Bus fare was cheap. Dating was done at church or Fellowship Club, so that didn't require cash. It was a big deal when I'd take my girl to Master's Restaurant for a Western sandwich. Butch never complained, though, and was understanding about my lack of finances.

"My folks have always been careful with their money," she commented.

"Well, even as a little kid, if I ever had any money, I had to earn it," I explained. "My principal source of income as a little shaver was Uncle Roll. He used to pay me a nickel or dime for shoveling his walk. Sometimes, if the snow was exceptionally deep, I'd even get fifteen cents, and I'd strut home feeling like a millionaire.

"My father always drummed conservative fiscal platitudes into me. 'Waste not, want not,' he would often remind me. 'If you spend it for something you don't need, that's wasting it,' he'd say. When I was in high school and worked at the A & P I'd make thirty-eight cents an hour. About eleven dollars a week. I'd take my pay home and put it in little envelopes marked for different purposes. When I start teaching I'll be able to have lots of little envelopes." I laughed.

"Are you going to take that job offer in Windsor?" she asked shyly.

"Not unless I absolutely have to. I want to stay in London." I grinned at her, paused dramatically, then added significantly, "For a number of reasons."

I knew my chances of being hired by the London school system weren't good, since they would only be taking on two or three new teachers. The morning the letter arrived from the board of education I was still snoozing. My mom called out, "Barry, your letter is here," and I was down the stairs in a flash. Still in my pajamas, I sat down on the living room floor and with quivering hands opened the envelope. "I'm afraid it's going to say 'sorry,'" Mom said, worried.

I glanced over the contents, gave out a whoop, and did a complete somersault there on the living room floor! Not only did I have a job, but it was in the city system, at Empress School. And Mr. Rex Fowler, my favorite teacher of all time, would be my principal! It was all I had dreamed of, and besides I would be paid the grand sum of $1,400 annually. The letter emphasized that teachers returning from the war would step into their respective niches in the seniority system, so I was a rookie of the rookies, but that seemed only right. The first year would be a sort of probationary period, but I didn't mind that either. I had my foot in the door, and come September, I'd have my very own class.

"But at nineteen, you won't be much older than some of

your students," Butch remarked when I told her the good news.

"I hadn't thought much about that."

"Do you think you'll have a hard time disciplining them?"

"Well, I guess I could use my father's ol' Rule of the Raised Finger."

"What?"

"Well, see, my father has always been the disciplinarian in our family, because I can usually sweet-talk my mother out of being angry with me. But my father, no way. When his finger went up in a menacing motion, that was a first warning. A second time—I'd better watch out. But if it was raised a third time, I'd had it.

"One time the four of us were visiting another church for some special meeting. We were sitting up in the balcony and there were some girls behind us I found quite distracting. Dad gave me a stern look, and up went his finger as if to say, 'That's one.' The temptation was too great, however, and I continued showing off for my appreciative audience. 'That's two,' he motioned. Despite the warnings, I persisted in amusing the giggling girls, and the ominous Finger of Fate indicated, 'That's three.'

"Then I got worried. I slid down in the pew, thinking, 'Maybe he'll forget if I'm really good the rest of the time.' During the streetcar ride home I kept praying he would have an unusual lapse of memory. He said nothing. We walked from the corner to our house, and up the porch steps. He slid the key into the lock, opened the door, and reached in to turn on the lights.

"'Barry, go to your room,' he told me quietly, and I went. He followed me shortly, carrying a wide leather razor strap. 'Son, you disobeyed me in church, and you know it. I'm going to have to punish you now.'

"'I won't do it again,' I promised.

"'I know you won't,' he agreed as he doubled that strap, and he gave me three good swats.

"'Now, pull your trousers up and finish crying,' he said kindly. 'Your punishment is over, but I don't want you to forget it.'

"He's never mentioned that incident again, but from

then on his raised finger had an amazing calming effect on me. I think he was fair with me. I knew what was expected of me, I was warned when I didn't measure up, and the punishment was appropriate. I hope I can handle my class as wisely."

I maintained this naive assumption until a couple of nights before school was to start. That evening I was warming up in the bullpen with catcher Gil Robertson when some toughs began heckling me from the top of the bleachers. "Hey, Barry! Who ever told you you could pitch?" "Just wait, Teach, you're going to get yours on Tuesday!" "Yeah, Chicken Wing, we'll see you in class. You won't last long. Just like on the mound!"

The realization that those cotton-pickers were going to be in my class unnerved me a bit. They were bigger than I was, and not much younger. I hoped they didn't know how old I was. I was looking forward to November when I'd no longer be a teenager.

Tuesday morning I reported for duty, shaking in my boots. Mr. Fowler, a very congenial, somewhat placid man, took me aside and explained in a confidential manner, "Barry, this is a tough class. Last year the boys ganged up on the teacher, knocked him down, and beat him severely. If you should have any trouble, use that first and explain it to me afterwards." I looked in the direction he had indicated. A baseball bat was propped up in the corner.

"Oh, I don't think I'll need that," I shook my head. After all, I was an athlete and in excellent shape. I certainly wasn't going to take any guff from a bunch of punks. "You can mark this down, Mr. Fowler. If one of them ever gets me down, I'm not going to stay down!"

"Good!"

I squared my shoulders, set my jaw in the most pugnacious position I could manage, and marched into that classroom as if I were really in charge. I looked around, and there were the bleacher bums sitting across the back row, slouched down in their seats. "I'm glad to see you here," I told them. "You guys are going to help run this class, and I'm going to make sure we run it the way you want it."

I walked over to the board and picked up a piece of chalk.

"OK, you make the rules. How should the class be run?" Hesitantly the class came up with some principles about classwork, deportment, and punishments. "OK," I declared, "that's the way she'll run. I want you to know that we are starting out even. I trust you, and you're not going to have any trouble with me, if you do what I ask you. You will be gentlemen. You will be courteous. If you aren't, you could have a burr by the tail."

They didn't really test my mettle until the second week of school, when one of our "gentlemen" got out of hand. I marched him to the principal's office, recorded the violation in the punishment book, and applied his three licks. When we got back to our second-floor classroom I expressed my sentiments to the class. "You kids aren't dumb. You all know what happened, and why. Rule number three was violated, and when rules are broken there is a price to pay. If you don't break the rules, everybody will stay happy and we'll have a lot of fun this year."

They weren't perfect the rest of the year, but we understood each other and got along quite well. The fact that I was called upon to serve as coach might have had something to do with that, because we did have a lot of fun on the playing field.

I was assigned the boys' hockey team, and started them off playing floor hockey until the weather could provide the needed ice. They seemed to enjoy this, and it gave them a head start on the rules and moves to use when we put on our skates.

After our first practice one of the smaller guys came up and asked, "Mr. Moore, where did you learn to play hockey?"

I wasn't used to the "Mr. Moore" bit, and he seemed so impressed, I had to grin at him. "Oh, when I was a little kid I played out on the street with a rubber ball with my friends. For a couple of years I lived right over there on Blackfriars." I gave a toss of my head, indicating the next street over from the school. "I used to roller skate up and down Blackfriars Street using a ball instead of a puck so I could practice my shots even if there was no ice.

"That winter my grandfather flooded the front yard so I

had my own private practice rink, and for Christmas I got my hockey equipment. I really worked at it. I had a lot of fun, and got to be pretty good. Why, a bunch of my friends and I got together one time and rented the London Arena for a challenge game with some kids from another school."

"You did what?" a couple of the kids asked in unison. As I warmed up to this story, more of the boys started joining the circle, all curious about how a bunch of kids could have played in the London Arena.

"Well, we found out that you could rent the place in the morning when no one else was using it for only ten dollars an hour. That was a lot of money to us, but we figured if we could get the other team to raise half of it, we could sell enough tickets at five cents apiece to come up with the ante. We cut pieces of cardboard and wrote ADMIT ONE— FIVE CENTS on them.

"We had been practicing over at Kensington Park, and even though we were a mixed bag—our ages were from about nine to twelve or thirteen, and I was the runt of the group—we felt we had a chance to win. Skating out on that ice that Saturday morning with the crowd yelling us on was the biggest thrill!

"I had been chosen to play goalie, and I was so scared I could hardly move. Those guys on the other team came out, and they all looked huge. They really were bigger than we were."

The boys listened breathlessly while I gave them a blow-by-blow description of the game. "And one of the big guys had one of those broken sticks with a hook in it, you know the kind?" They all shook their heads. "Well, he whipped a shot from center ice right at me. I can see that puck coming yet! I was so tense, my legs wouldn't move, and plunk! Right into the net."

"Did you win?"

"No, we lost, five to three. But it was a fun game. I've played on a lot of teams since then, and have gotten a bit of experience. I was goalie for the team that won the Juvenile Boys' Hockey Championship in 1943."

After that the boys took any suggestions or corrections

I'd make about the game. That is, most of them did.

That October another challenging opportunity came my way. Ken Welch had planned a big area-wide youth rally to be held at the Beal Tech High School Auditorium. Bern Corrin, the regular song leader for the Saturday night fellowship gatherings, was a med student and wouldn't be available that Thursday. Could I do it?

Could I? I wasn't really sure. The largest group I'd led in singing was the Sunday night crowd at Wortley Church, but they were expecting 800 or 900 people for the rally. In the past year or so I had had numerous opportunities to lead small groups, but was I really ready for the big time? I hesitated a moment, reminded myself that I had gotten into this to serve the Lord, then, using my most confident voice, responded, "Sure, Ken, I'll be glad to do that for you."

The night of the big event I got all decked out in my new, blue double-breasted suit with wide lapels. It was the latest thing. My hair was slicked back just so with the pompadour on the left side. If it hadn't been for my sweaty palms, dry mouth, and queasy stomach, everything would have been fine. As the auditorium began filling I wondered what I had gotten myself into. I paced up and down, as nervous as I would be before a championship match.

The attendance exceeded everyone's expectations. They had reporters down front interviewing people and photographers taking pictures. Even Mr. Fowler, my principal, was there. This was without doubt the biggest Christian gathering in London for some time. I got up and announced the first song, and, just as in an athletic event, I found that once I started, it was OK. I could channel my energies into swinging my arms and arousing the enthusiasm of the crowd. It was a great night.

After that, whenever Corrin wasn't available, Ken would have me lead singing on Saturday nights. Because he was also responsible for raising funds, Ken would often get Audrey and me to accompany him and his wife Betty to various churches to present the work and needs of the Fellowship Club. I'd lead the singing, we'd have some young people sing a duet or something for special music, and Ken would preach. The four of us became good friends and the Welches were soon aware of the fact that Butch and I had an "agreement."

It wasn't until New Year's Eve that the "agreement" became official. I figured that would be a great way to start 1946 off in style, but wanted it to be a surprise for Butch. We went to the usual Watch Night service at Wortley Church and enjoyed the goodies that had been produced in the huge old stove in the basement kitchen.

When the services broke up shortly after the New Year had begun, I was still rarin' to go. "My folks will still be up," I told Butch, "C'mon over to my house for a while." It was freezing cold, but typically, she agreed to hike the mile and a half over to my home, even though it meant a two-mile walk home later. We laughed and sang and teased on the way over and it seemed no distance at all. She never complained. She was my kind of gal!

We got inside the house and took off our coats. "Wait just a minute, will you? I want to show you something." I dashed up the stairs to my room. Then I came down and grabbed her hand. "Say, you don't want to wear this old cameo I gave you, do you?" She looked startled as I pulled it off her finger. "Wouldn't you rather wear this?" I asked and held out a diamond.

"Oh!" she gasped as I placed it on her finger. She grinned and kind of hugged herself. And then I hugged her. We went next door to my grandfather's where my folks were waiting for us.

No one seemed surprised at the announcement, although the Snelgroves were rather unenthusiastic about losing their only daughter. "We aren't going to get married until I finish university," I assured them. We were both quite young, but mature enough to realize it would be better to wait until I finished the degree. That would mean I was in line for a principalship one day.

Deciding to ask Butch to marry me hadn't been as hard a decision as the one facing me the next spring. When hockey season was over and I was put in charge of the boys' baseball team, my fancy turned to thoughts of pitching for the Majors again. My record for the past year pretty much assured me that I could make the team if I tried. They had given me a hard time before because I couldn't practice on Sundays. Now I had the young people's meetings on Saturday night to consider. Could I really put Christ first in my life and play ball too?

The desire to return to the mound was strong, but it boiled down to a choice between pitching or leading singing. There was no way I could do both. One Saturday night that spring Audrey and I were walking toward the meeting hall, and when we came to the corner of Richmond and Fullerton Streets, I paused and looked toward the river. The floodlights of the ball park were shining brightly, and I knew all the guys were down there getting ready for a game. I stood there with the lights beckoning to me. Fullerton Street led to the ball park; Richmond Street to the youth meeting. I recalled the night I had made my commitment. There was only one decision I could make. Resolutely, I took Audrey's arm and we crossed Fullerton and continued up Richmond to the auditorium.

"Ken does a good job of finding speakers," I mentioned to Butch on the walk home. "He mixes pastors, evangelists, and Bible teachers so that we don't have the same type of meeting each time."

"And of course you are a connoisseur of preaching?" she teased.

"Well, I ought to be. I've been exposed to enough preaching in my life. My folks always enjoyed visiting other churches to hear special speakers, and would often invite the preachers or evangelists into our home. Matter of fact, Wilbur Cedarholm from Waterloo, Iowa, was one of the early influences in my life. He was quite a guy. He not only preached, but played the guitar, the piano, and glasses with varying amounts of water in them. You know what I mean?"

She nodded assurance.

"Yeah, well, he stayed in our guest room for three or four weeks, and I got to ply him with questions. He never did give me the impression that I was bothering him, although I must have been a pest. I remember he had a silly song he used to sing about a man who was so thin that he fell through a hole in the seat of his pants and choked to death. He patiently sang that over and over for me.

"Another time James McGinley, the famous radio preacher, came to our home. I was just a little shaver, but I was so impressed. I sat on the floor looking up at the platinum-haired Scotsman, listening to the same pleasing brogue that came rolling out of our radio Sunday after Sunday. I was really mesmerized, and sat there staring while he played with one of our kittens, sipping the tea Mother had served him.

"There were a number of preachers who stayed in our 'prophet's chamber.' They were all kind to me and seemed to take an interest in me."

"That means a lot to a little kid," Audrey commented.

"Yeah, and it means a lot to me that you are interested in me, too."

She grinned, and looked very pleased.

"I'm going to sign up for as many courses as I can possibly carry at the university this summer. Got to get that degree so I can marry my gal."

FOUR
MY DAY IN COURT

With great incentive, I really applied myself to my courses that summer, and did well. My year of probationary teaching was completed, so I began the fall semester of 1946 as a full-fledged staff member. I was fully confident that I could handle the class this year, after having established my reputation the year before.

Because of my athletic involvement over the years, I had become well known among local sports enthusiasts. I'd also gotten a bit of publicity because of my song leading for the youth rallies. Being well known in my little fish pond made me feel quite self-assured.

I wasn't surprised, therefore, when one of the grade eight boys approached me and asked if I would address a youth group. I'd never preached a sermon before, but it seemed a natural next step in serving the Lord. I produced an outline that seemed a sure winner, and practiced it diligently. Feeling confident I was prepared to impress the entire Oak Street Corps of the Salvation Army, I ventured forth on what was sure to be an auspicious occasion.

In spite of my arrogance, the Lord used my words that night. I was certain of it, for everyone there listened intently. All nine of them.

Another comedown for my pride came when I had a run-in with one of the "gentlemen" at school. This kid had a lousy attitude from day one. I think he was trying to live up to the reputation of his older brother, but I wasn't going to take any lip from him no matter how tough he thought he was.

Our hockey team was scheduled to play St. George's, so I got the guys all together and handed out two streetcar passes to each player. "Now remember, we're to travel together," I reminded the group and reviewed the standards of conduct the school had for outings such as this. "Now, get your equipment together and we'll meet at the front of the school."

Well, Charlie couldn't pass up such an opportunity to rebel. He got his gear and dashed down to the corner. The rest of us were just assembling when this bus goes by with Charlie on it. He was making faces and giving us the raspberry as he rode off, thinking he was going to be the first up at St. George's. I motioned for him to get off the bus, but he just shrugged and turned up his nose at me. What smart-aleck Charlie didn't know was I had just gotten a call from St. George's saying their rink wasn't in shape, and the game had been cancelled.

The rest of the boys were all geared up and ready to play, so we checked the ice at Kensington Park where we practiced, and it was fine. An hour or so later we were about to finish playing, when up struts Charlie with a cigarette dangling out of his mouth. He proceeds to the center of the rink and yells at me, "What the h--- do you think you're pullin' off?"

That irritated my Irish a bit, but I just said, "Charlie, before we discuss this, take that cigarette out of your mouth."

"I'm not taking this cigarette out of my mouth for you or any other blankety-blank."

"Charlie, you are on school property, and the rules say you cannot smoke on school property!" Somewhere in the back of my mind a voice seemed to say, *"That's two."*

"I'm going to smoke here, and you're not going to stop me."

"Charlie, take it out of your mouth, or I'll take it out."
"Try it!"

That was the third warning, and I'd had it. With one long swooping movement, I knocked the offending object out of his mouth. He grabbed at me. I knew his brother had been in on beating my predecessor, but I wasn't going to let it become a family tradition. Before he knew what happened, I had my arm around his neck in a hammerlock.

He was swinging and flailing around trying to get at me, but he couldn't break my hold. The rules said I couldn't hit him, but they didn't mention choking, so I just held on. He cussed and swore and called me every name in the book. When he'd had enough, I let him go and yelled, "You get out of here. Now! We'll talk tomorrow at school."

"I'm going to get my brother," he screamed. "And my old man. And-and we'll take you to court. . . ." He was so livid, he was foaming at the mouth.

After I'd dismissed the rest of the team and had a moment to consider what had transpired, I got a mite worried. After all, I was still new at teaching. I didn't have any tenure or pull with the school board. Maybe his father could get me in trouble. When I got home I put in a call to Mr. Fowler and explained to him exactly what had happened.

"Don't worry about it, Barry. I know that family and I'll stand with you. We may have to go to court, but that's all right, we'll win that battle, too. You have a good supper."

The next day Charlie's father appeared at school. He proved to be a stubborn, hard-nosed businessman who seemed to think his boys didn't have to obey the same rules as the others. And we wound up in court!

Talk about being deflated! I'd never been in a courtroom in my life, and this was a very solemn situation. The white-haired judge looked as stern and foreboding as an Old Testament prophet. He sat there in stony-faced silence while the lawyer for the plaintiff made me sound like Genghis Khan. Then Mr. Fowler went to bat for me, explaining the history of trouble the school had had with the family, and my performance as a teacher.

The judge turned to me and asked in his gravelly voice, "Did you hit this boy?"

"No sir. School law says that you can't hit the boy."

Left to right:
My early days of
sports—1941.

My summers were
devoted to
baseball—1944.

Audrey playing golf
with me in 1947.
What a stance!

Our wedding. Mom
and Dad Snelgrove,
Barry and Audrey,
Mom and Dad
Moore—1948.

"Did you touch him?"

"Yes, sir," I admitted. "I had him around the neck. I restrained him. He grabbed at me first, and I took him around the neck to hold him off."

"You didn't hit him?" he persisted.

"No, sir."

"But you were choking him pretty good?"

"Yes, sir. I sure was."

The judge fought a losing battle to hold back a smile at that response. Then came what seemed like the world's longest pause. Finally he turned and looked straight at Charlie's father.

"Stand up!" he thundered.

The father stood to his feet.

"I've had the last of your family in court. I'm only going to tell you this one time, my friend. If one of your boys appears in my court again for any misdemeanor, I'll lock you up." And he hit his desk with such a whack I thought it would split in two. "Do you understand that?" he demanded.

The father was visibly shaken. He nodded his head.

Bang! went the judge's gavel. "Case dismissed."

There were no more problems with that family. No sass from any of the boys. From then on they said "Mr. Moore" with a different tone of voice.

Then a real crisis occurred. The Snelgroves had been fussing at me for keeping Audrey out too late, but it's hard to say good-night to such a sweetheart. "She's over-tired," her mother would complain. When she got a sore throat and took to her bed, I became concerned.

The doctor was called and at first diagnosed her case as the flu, but when she continued to get worse, he seemed uncertain. She had been flat in bed for two weeks when I got a call from Mr. Snelgrove late one night. "Barry, I thought you would want to know. Dr. Fraser has called for an ambulance to take Audrey to St. Joseph's Hospital. He's putting her in isolation, so she won't be able to have any visitors. He's not sure, but he thinks she might have diphtheria."

Massive doses of diphtheria serum disproved that theory and left her with a rash, on top of her roaring fever. They began pumping penicillin into her, still giving us little real information and leaving me very anxious about her condition.

After school let out in the afternoons, I would walk over the Blackfriars Bridge to St. Joseph's Hospital and I'd pace up and down in front of the stark, white-brick, mausoleum-looking building, praying that God would restore her to health. I couldn't help but feel that she would get better a lot sooner if only I were allowed to see her. It was so totally frustrating to be barred from her room. This was the girl God had given to me, and I wasn't allowed to even see her while she was hovering near death's door!

After ninety-nine shots of the antibiotic, she finally passed the crisis. Two weeks after she entered St. Joseph's, she was discharged, and I got to see her. She looked so pitiful I realized just how close she had been to dying. She'd always been a little slip of a girl, but now she was downright puny looking. At least with her home I could hover around and fetch and carry things to her.

It took weeks for her to regain her strength, and the whole incident made me rethink this idea of waiting until I received my degree before we married. Going to night school and in the summers, even taking as heavy a load as possible, it would still be years before we could marry. I considered her my girl, and I wanted the rest of the world to concede that fact. Why, an article about me that appeared in the Canadian Youth Fellowship's *Youth In Action* paper had even said, "Sorry, girls, but he's engaged!" Now that's the way it was supposed to be. We belonged to each other.

The big event of the summer of 1947 was the merging of the Canadian Youth Fellowship with Youth For Christ International. The organizations had begun as a simultaneous movement of the Spirit of God among young people on the North American continent. It seemed only natural that we should forge ahead under one banner, since our purposes were identical.

To make this event even more exciting to me personally, I was privileged to attend the Keswick Conference that summer and be exposed to all the excitement. Leading singing for that crowd, with Tedd Smith at the keyboard, was tantamount to a trip to heaven. The Spirit of God had breathed life into this evangelistic movement, and I was privileged to be a spectator to it.

I returned to London with renewed zeal. I taught school by day, attended classes a couple of nights a week, and on Saturday mornings. I was involved at Wortley Church on Sundays, and my spare time was all devoted to Youth For Christ. When my devoted bride-to-be couldn't be involved with me, she sat home and knitted me argyle socks, crocheted, and sewed fancy doo-dads to fill the cedar chest I had gotten for her birthday. I considered it a blessing to have a fianceé who not only understood my priorities, but encouraged me in them.

Late that fall I was invited to lead singing in Toronto for the Fellowship Baptist Young People's Association and boarded the Canadian National coach heading northeast. As I walked down the aisle I was delighted to spot a familiar face.

"Gordie Tapp! How in the world are you doing?" I chortled, giving him a whack on the back.

"Barry! Good to see you. It's been a while since our days in The Booth."

"Yeah. Remember Norman Scoyne's Sunday school class at Briscoe Church?"

"Couldn't forget, or the way he would crack our knee caps if we cut up. Remember the church picnics when we used to all load up on the back of a Belton Brothers' truck to go to Springbank Park? You always had to sing louder than the rest of us. 'One door and only one, and yet its sides are two.' You always liked that one."

"Right. And the 'sword drills.'"

"You would mention that, Barry, because you always beat me. You were an energetic little cuss."

"Well, you've been doing all right for yourself, too. You really got the bug for entertaining while you were in the Army, eh?"

"Well, it started in Nova Scotia, when I won the Canadian Army Amateur contest. I just did the same ol' impersonations I used to do at The Booth. Donald Duck, Walter

Winchell, Amos and Andy. Same routine. When I was discharged, the Department of Veterans' Affairs paid my way
to the Academy of Radio Arts that Lorne Green had just
opened. I got my first job as a deejay in Niagara Falls,
Ontario. Then I went to Guelph, to Hamilton, and now I'm
signing on with CBC."

"That really sounds exciting, Gordie. I'm teaching school
at Empress, where I attended a couple of years as a kid."

"That's not all you've been doing. I read in the papers
every once in a whole about you appearing with Youth For
Christ at this place or that. As a deejay I've read announcements about your activities. It makes me feel kind of proud
that I know a young man who is carrying on the Lord's
work."

"I really appreciate that, Gordie. You know . . . ." Our
spirited conversation made that one of the shortest trips I
ever took from London to Toronto.

All the opportunities that were opening for me to lead
singing, or speak, or even do some solo work, were exciting,
but they really kept me on the run. I finally decided that if I
was going to have much time with Butch, we'd have to get
married. Soon. She agreed, and we set the date for the
following spring—June 26, 1948.

This decision kept all the females in my life—Audrey and
her mother, and my mother and sister—aflutter with plans
for months. While they worried about momentous things
like who would wear what, I was concerned about practical
decisions such as finding a home.

Ken Welch had already decided he would be returning to
Chatham in the spring, so he agreed to rent Butch and me
his house at 18 Bellvue Avenue. One advantage of having
gone together for four and a half years was that we had
both been saving our money and were able to buy new
furniture. We picked out living room, dining room, kitchen,
and bedroom furniture. There were a couple of extra bedrooms in the house and I stuck an old desk and some
books in one of them. As the day drew near, the presents
rolled in, helping us fix up our new home. We were even
given a grocery shower by the church.

We decided that we would keep our honeymoon plans a

big secret. Since we were going to fly, we had to let it be known that we would be needing a ride to the airport, and when people started presuming that we were going to attend the Youth For Christ Convention at Winona Lake, Indiana, we didn't say anything. I wasn't about to take my bride there, though. That would be a mob scene, and I wanted to have her all to myself.

The big day dawned bright, clear, and hot. Sunshine blazed through the glorious stained glass windows of Wortley Church, highlighted the new wine-colored carpeting, and warmed the rich wood of the pews and trim in the beautiful gothic sanctuary.

Ken Browne began playing an organ prelude, and Pastor Dunkin called me aside just before we were to go out into the auditorium for the ceremony. On such a solemn occasion as this I expected some really profound advice from the man who was not only my minister, but a friend. "Look, Barry," he said in a loud stage whisper, "if you faint, fall the other way, don't fall on me!"

Ken Welch, who was serving as my best man, cracked up. I'll have to admit to being a bit of a prankster myself, but I thought teasing me at a time like that was a little much. Harry McKenzie and Don Marshall were serving as ushers, so at least they were busy out front and couldn't give me a hard time.

My Uncle Albert sang "The Lord's Prayer" and "Because," and it was time for us to line up. Ken began playing the wedding march, and the bridesmaids started down the aisle. Then I saw my bride gliding toward me. She looked lovely. The sunlight made her satiny gown almost iridescent as she floated down the aisle with her dress and veil trailing behind her. Then as she was turning the corner by the front, her gown caught on a pew. I felt a flash of panic, but her mother reached over and coolly loosened the gown she had sewed with such loving care.

John Dunkin threw us a curve during the exchanging of the vows by including a phrase he hadn't used in the rehearsal, but I liked the addition. With a sense of anticipation I vowed to be faithful to my wife "until Jesus comes, or death do us part."

52

After all the congratulations, picture taking, and a good deal of teasing, we headed to the Snelgroves' so Butch could change for our trip. When she came down the stairs in her strawberry-colored traveling outfit with white hat and corsage, she looked so good I think I fell in love all over again.

"Doesn't our little girl look nice?" her mother asked poignantly.

"Absolutely terrific!"

We made a mad dash for the airport, and I felt mighty pleased to be flying off on a romantic trip with my bride. It was the first flight for both of us. Matter of fact, I didn't even know many people who had ever flown. We boarded the flight, the stewardess took one look at us and said, "Oh, you've just been married, haven't you?"

We landed in Windsor, about 100 miles away as the DC-3 flies, and boarded a bus for our ultimate destination—Port Elgin. After a half hour or so we entered Chatham.

"Chatham!" Butch exclaimed. "We're headed right back to London!"

We did some checking and discovered that our flight to Windsor had taken us in the wrong direction. I'd been so pleased with myself for coming up with the idea of flying that I hadn't bothered to look on a map. So I wasted some capital. And some time. But we didn't care. We had a ball.

When our week was over, Audrey was anxious to get back to our own place. She seems to have a strong nesting instinct, and I was rather looking forward to using all our lovely new possessions myself. We reached the front door, I smiled down at her, and in a romantic haze we opened "our" front door. We could not enter the room because of all the toilet paper streamers hanging everywhere. Our gang— I hesitate to call them friends—had gotten into the house and rolled it, but good. We had to break through streamers to make our way around to discover just how much damage they had done. Dirt was spread all over the floor. There was an old tire in the living room. They'd made a fake bonfire. Someone had gotten an old wooden golf club and attached a sign saying, "No more fun!"

We went into the dining room, and the table had been set

with all our new dishes. Names had been set at each place. They had my name at the head of the table, Audrey's at the foot, and about eight kids' names were lined up at the sides. In the kitchen we discovered they had taken every label off our cans of food. We dreaded going upstairs. They'd been there too. A tire had been stuffed between the mattress and the springs on the bed. Toilet paper was strung everywhere. The bed clothes were all messed up. It took us all afternoon to get the place back in order.

"What shall we do to them?" Butch grinned with a mischievous look in her eye.

We couldn't come up with any way to get them back *en masse*, so I suggested we just give them the silent treatment.

"The silent treatment?"

"That means you just ignore them. Pretend that nothing happened, and leave them wondering."

Just before school began, Butch and I attended the Keswick Youth For Christ Camp. I'd been there the year before, but it was a lot more fun with a wife along. It was also very inspirational, with Robert Barr of Toronto giving the devotions each morning, and Charles Templeton, J. D. Carlson, Billy Graham, and Jack Scott conducting the evening meetings.

A highlight for me was a pickup softball game in which I got to pitch against both Billy Graham and Chuck Templeton. Billy hit cross-handed, and I struck him out. Chuck got a single off me, but if it had been a hardball he never would have seen it. Afterward I had an opportunity to share with Templeton that I had made a decision in one of his meetings as a boy, and now I really wanted to serve the Lord.

"That's great, Barry," he responded. He kicked the dirt with the toe of his sneaker a bit, then sighed and looked off into the horizon. "You know, Barry, I've preached to ten people and I've preached to 10,000 people, and I'm still not satisfied."

The restive spirit that he demonstrated puzzled me. Chuck Templeton was a big wheel in Youth For Christ. He'd been chosen as the first regional vice-president for

Eastern Canada and had been on the first team to go to Europe. Yet he seemed troubled.

What troubled me was that with Ken and Betty Welch living in Chatham there was no one spearheading the work in the London area. Ken served as lifeguard at the Camp, so we got to be together some. "Everyone has looked to you for leadership since you started the work, Ken. I just don't know how it will go without you," I confided.

Ken gave me one of his slow grins and a knowing look crossed his face as he prophesied, "Oh, I think the Lord will raise up someone to take my place."

Top: Riot in Brussels, Belgium, when King Leopold was forced to abdicate.

Bottom: The Canadians at the Belgium Congress of 1950: I'm third from the right, top row.

FIVE
INNOCENTS
ABROAD

As fall turned into winter, Welch's rating as a prophet dropped as rapidly as the attendance at the rallies. The young man who had inherited the position of president of London's Youth For Christ was obviously in over his head. He soon discovered there was a lot more to it than inviting someone to speak. The nitty-gritty details of financial support, booking musicians, providing accommodations, and publicizing the meetings were overwhelming to this novice.

I was placed in an awkward position by being elected vice-president to serve under him. The thinning of the crowds and lack-luster atmosphere at the rallies were distressing not only to me, but to other leaders in the group. "Let's give him some time," one of the older fellows counseled. "Perhaps he will catch on."

When I was asked to take charge of a meeting in February, I decided to try to liven things up a bit. I'd heard Billy Graham preach a number of times at Keswick and thought the folks might enjoy hearing him. With Jack Van Impe and his accordian for special music and a little extra publicity we drew 900 people that night.

Since I had responsibility for Graham while he was in London, I invited him to spend the afternoon in our home. While he rested upstairs on our bed, I told Butch I never wanted to be an evangelist.

"Why not?"

"Look at Graham. He's tired out. Just got back from a trip to Germany, on the road all the time, never gets to be with his wife, and she's raising their kids alone. No. I'd never want to be an evangelist. No way."

It seemed to me that I was busy enough—teaching during the day, taking night classes at the university, singing with the Volunteer Quartet, teaching Sunday school, and leading singing at the Youth For Christ rallies.

"And you're supposed to spend some time with me," Butch reminded me.

"Oh, yeah. Gotta make time for you."

Shortly after that I caught a bug and wound up flat on my back with a severely painful throat and a fever. I'd always been so healthy that I was certain I was about to die. Doc Fraser came over, stuffed a thermometer in my mouth, and while he was taking my pulse cheerily announced, "Well, I've checked your wife, and you're going to be a father. I'm very happy for you."

"That's great," I moaned. It really was. I was thrilled, but it was rather difficult to express my excitement under those circumstances.

I spent two weeks in bed. My recovery was complete, but Butch had a while to go yet. She continued to work until April, and then, as was customary, she quit when she started wearing maternity clothes.

When our year's lease was up on the Welches' house, they decided they wanted to sell it. We didn't want to buy it, however, because my folks had given us a lot next door to their home as a wedding gift. We wanted to build our own little love nest on Langarth Street where my roots were.

So here I was with a very pregnant wife and the necessity of finding new living quarters near my new assignment at Princess Elizabeth School and Wortley Church. When this proved difficult, my in-laws came to the rescue by inviting us to live with them until after the baby came. Besides helping us out, I think they rather enjoyed the idea of hovering over their only daughter as the blessed event neared.

During the summer months the YFC rallies had continued to drag. When we got down to about twenty-five, the diehards who were still hanging in there began putting pressure on me to take the leadership. I talked over the possibility with Butch, who wasn't all that enthusiastic about the prospect.

"But you are so busy already," she pointed out. "How could you find time to take on such a big responsibility?"

"I don't know. But think about it. It kinda seems that the Lord has been preparing me for this. First I got experience working in Sunday school assemblies. That prepared me for serving as president of the Literary Society at Normal School. The experience in the Literary Society prepared me for taking responsibility for assemblies at Empress School. Teaching and leading singing got me over being afraid of being before crowds, so that now I can speak without falling apart. Also, the time spent running around with Ken Welch to all the area rallies gave me an opportunity to pick up a lot of tips from him."

"You really feel you should do this?"

"Well, doesn't it seem to you that God has been preparing me for something? And who is better qualified?"

"I guess you're right," she sighed. "It's just that I know you so well. You can't do anything halfway, and if you take on the responsibility for Youth For Christ, I'll never see you."

"But it's OK with you?"

"How can I say no if you feel that's what the Lord wants you to do?"

"You are beautiful," I exclaimed and gave her a big kiss.

"Yeah, sure," she laughed, looking at her oversized tummy. It really was amazing to me how a ninety-eight-pound weakling could become so out of proportion. That baby was going to be a whopper.

Shortly after I was elected president of London YFC, Harry McKenzie, Ralph Hamilton, and I went over to Russell Winslow's home for a serious discussion. Mr. Winslow, a senior officer with Canada Trust, was an older man we all respected and affectionately called "Uncle Bus."

"What seems to be the problem, Barry?" he asked.

"Well, I'm supposed to be president now. But president of

what? There's not much left. It seems to me there's going to have to be a drastic change of direction. First we need to ask ourselves, is there really a need for Youth For Christ in London?"

Uncle Bus leaned back, stroked his chin thoughtfully, then replied. "As long as there are young people, there is a need."

"OK, then that's our challenge, but we're going to have to get moving. If you men are behind me, then I've got some ideas."

"Fine. We'll back you," was the consensus.

"OK. First we're going to have to get a board of responsible businessmen who can give us some organizational strength. We need to involve more churches, and more denominations; this isn't just a fellowship of Baptists and Brethren. Also we need to enlist a group of regular supporters to put us on a more solid financial basis. I've got my income from teaching, so I don't need any compensation for my time, but there are expenses involved in running an operation the size this should be. Then we need to plan a big rally. Something to give us a shot in the arm as we try to revitalize our program." The words came rushing out in a torrent. I had enough ideas to keep us busy for at least a year, but they agreed on the first four and pledged to help.

Harry took on the responsibility of advertising. That took a big load off me, because I knew that he was the kind of guy that, if he said he was behind you, you could depend on.

We talked Muriel Barrie, the organist at Wortley, into becoming our first secretary. She claimed she didn't know what she was doing, and had had no secretarial experience, but I figured that if I could bluff my way through, so could she. "Twink" was a spunky gal who was willing to try.

Next we needed a dedicated treasurer. I didn't know whom to collar for that position, so I decided to make that a matter of prayer while concentrating on producing an outstanding rally. I got going and lined up Jack Scott, who had served as co-director of Toronto YFC. He was well known in Youth For Christ circles and I figured he would be a real draw.

Then I got permission to use the Central Baptist Church to free us from paying rent for a secular auditorium. I rented a short film, secured some special music, and prayed!

I was the first one there for the big night. I paced up and down like a caged lion, figuring this would be good practice for impending fatherhood. My prayer was simple: "Lord, I've done all I can, now it's up to you to bless." That was the only way I knew to run the show.

People started trickling in. I got busy talking with the musicians, making sure everyone understood where to be when, so that the program would move smoothly. I checked the crowd, and the place was packed. There must have been 700 or 800 people there. I swallowed hard and mumbled, "Thank you, Lord." The turnout and the enthusiasm the crowd exhibited seemed to be the Lord's endorsement of my efforts. There was no holding me down after that.

What little time I spent at home those weeks, I was on the phone calling anyone and everyone I thought could give me the guidance and encouragement I needed. I phoned Martin DeHaan, Charles Fuller, Torrey Johnson. I figured I might as well start at the top. Bob Cook agreed to come and speak, and that was a real shot in the arm. It seemed as if everyone had been holding back, waiting for someone to show some modicum of leadership and enthusiasm. When I became willing for the Lord to use me in that capacity, the logjam was broken and young people and adults alike made themselves available for service.

About the third rally I conducted I was sitting on the platform during the sermon looking over the crowd, when my eye spotted Dick Dengate. Dick was a born-again, dedicated member of the United Church of Canada. "There's our treasurer," I thought. I cornered him after the meeting and decided to use a subtle approach.

"Dick, do you want to put God first in your life?"

"Well, well, you know I do," he stammered.

"Then I want you to serve as our treasurer."

He proved to be a cold, calculating, precise keeper of the

purse strings. Just what we needed. "If you've only got thirty-five dollars in the bank, you can't spend fifty dollars!" he insisted. "And if you are going to bring in all these speakers and musical talent from all over, you're going to have to figure a way to pay their expenses."

We started booking our speakers in various churches on Sundays to help pay the freight. I guess we ran them kind of ragged, but they didn't run any harder than we did.

Finally, the evening of October 20, I checked Butch into Victoria Hospital. The doctor came out and informed me, "There's nothing doing yet. Go on home and get some sleep. We'll call you as soon as there is any progress."

That was a frustrating pronouncement. I wanted to be near Audrey, but it didn't seem sensible to spend the night in the waiting room for nothing. With another promise from the nurse, I went on home to fellowship with the mattress.

The next morning I was assured that it was safe for me to go ahead and teach my class. If there was any progress, they would call me. That day I learned the meaning of the expression "being on pins and needles." I kept expecting to be called to the phone, but nothing happened. As soon as class was dismissed, I hurried to the hospital. But after hours of waiting, I was again convinced to go home and get a good night's sleep.

By ten o'clock I was sound asleep, only to be awakened by the ringing of the phone. "Your wife's in labor. We've taken her into delivery." I got over there in less time than it takes to tell, took the elevator to the maternity floor, and stepped out to find Junior Resident Donald Marshall grinning from ear to ear.

"Don, what's the word?" Somehow it seemed very special to have a member of our wedding party in on the birth of our first child.

"C'mon over to the nursery and I'll introduce you to your daughter," he announced.

"Daughter?"

"Nine pounds, four ounces. A real little beauty. And Audrey is just fine," he added, anticipating my next question.

I wasn't allowed in the nursery, but they had a big glassed-in window for viewing. Don went in and wheeled one of the little beds up to the glass, picked up a pink little bundle, and held her for me to see. I felt a little weak in the knees. Proud. Glad. Thankful. Weepy. To realize that precious little baby was my daughter. What a miracle!

Don was laughing his head off in there. I guess my mixed emotions must have been showing on my face. I was just so relieved that she was all right, and Audrey had survived. To think of a little gal like mine producing such a large offspring was mind-boggling. I had so much to be thankful for.

When it came time to bring Kerry Jane and her mom home, my in-laws came in their brand new maroon Ford. I wouldn't go so far as to say they bought the car just to bring their granddaughter home from the hospital, but it was evident from day one that Kerry Jane was going to have her share of affection from both sets of first-time grandparents.

Shortly after our daughter was installed in her little crib in our room, we had another addition to our family. An alpine blue Ford sedan, my very first car. It was tough for me to take the financial plunge, but it was very evident that I could not adequately serve as director of YFC and catch a bus everywhere I needed to go. I'll have to admit it was exhilarating to slip behind the wheel of my shiny new vehicle and feel all that horsepower jump to my command.

As the new decade dawned we were running full steam at the Youth For Christ rallies—sometimes quite literally.

One time we featured the Old Fashioned Revival Hour Quartet. We not only packed out Beal Tech's auditorium that night, but the gymnasium as well. We pulled that off by some fancy scheduling and a lot of running up and down stairs. While announcements were being made upstairs, the quartet was singing downstairs. We juggled the offerings and other special music the same way, and the quartet was panting by the time Merv Rosell started preaching in the auditorium and Roy Gustafson in the gymnasium.

When Bob Cook, then president of Youth For Christ International, came to London I rather selfishly booked him to speak at Wortley Church on Sunday night. I wanted to share the witty, personable preacher with my home folks. Cook had not only been one of the founding fathers of YFCI, but one of the first to take the message of Christ around the world under that banner. The fact that he had started out as a song leader made him appeal to me even more.

The fire marshall would have had a fit if he had seen how overcrowded our building was that night. From the way they responded during the song service it was easy to tell this was a turned-on crowd. They weren't disappointed by the speaker either. Bob was all wound up about the response he had seen in various countries in the world. "And this summer we want to send 500 men into Europe to reinstate the gospel," he thundered. Then he whirled around, looked our pastor straight in the eye, and said, "Dunkin, you ought to go! Get a team together and go!"

The challenge stunned the crowd a bit as it ricochetted around the sanctuary, but it hit me dead center. "You could go and lead the singing," came the startling thought. "All you would need would be a musician." Sitting there on the platform, I glanced about the congregation until my eye stopped on Lyall Conlin. Lyall was a student at the London Bible Institute. He played for our YFC rallies. He played both piano and organ, sang a bit, and could make his accordion talk.

The three of us would make a great team, but the thought of leaving my girls didn't appeal to me. Kerry Jane was only a few months old, but she had so much personality already it was amazing. She had me so charmed that the thought of missing out on her first summer gave me an empty feeling. And Butch. We'd never been separated. I'd grown accustomed to having her around, and surely didn't like the idea of leaving her for such a length of time.

Yet it would be more practical for me than for most men, since as a school teacher I had the summer months off. The other 499 men would have to leave their families, too. Was I willing to make the sacrifice? The conflicting thoughts raced through my head. "Well, Lord," I finally prayed, "if this is of you, then open the doors and I'll go."

Both Dunkin and Conlin were excited about the prospective venture. Butch, bless her heart, was unenthusiastic, but willing. Our parents seemed to think I'd really gone off the deep end this time, but didn't try to stop me. The Snelgroves did insist that if I was going to be gone the whole summer, Audrey and the baby should stay with them.

Responsibility for raising the monstrous sum of $3,300 to fund the trip fell to me. I set up a round of deputation-type meetings and, often accompanied by the Volunteer Quartet, beat the bushes seeking supporters who would pray as well as give. Just as the last of the needed backers were stepping forth, Dunkin opted out. I mean, just because his wife was due to deliver in July. What kind of an excuse was that? I was glad Conlin was single.

When I informed YFCI of the problem, they suggested Ken Welch. My old buddy! He agreed, and the team of Welch, Moore, and Conlin was assigned to leave for France on June 20, 1950.

I'd studied French all through high school, and had had another year at the university, but had spent more time learning to conjugate verbs than in actual conversation. That background had to be better than nothing. I got hold of a French hymnal and practiced leading singing in French and worked on a few solos.

To save money Conlin and I decided we'd go by boat. Welch couldn't leave until later, so he was to fly and meet us in Paris. Butch drove us to Quebec where we were to board the *R.M.S. Samaria* of the Cunard White Star Line. After a weepy farewell scene with my wife, we lugged our stuff on board and down to our "luxury" cabin, E-11.

Now Lyall Conlin is a rather mild-mannered fellow, the perfect introvert to offset my extrovertedness. The problem is he seemed so modest and withdrawn compared to me that no one would ever blame him for any tomfoolery that went on during the week-long trip. But he got in his licks.

I recall one night one of our cabin mates, Carl Purdy, made the mistake of coming in late. The rest of us tied his pajamas in knots and short-sheeted his bed, then jumped into our bunks and pretended we were asleep. He tiptoed in considerately and proceeded to strip down to his dahlia-covered shorts, then reached under his pillow for his PJs. They were one big grotesque lump. "Well, hallelujah!" he shouted. "Good night! Lord, deliver me!" And he let out a loud, good-natured guffaw. "All right, you crackers! Which one of you tied up my pajamas?"

Naturally we all feigned innocence. Purdy's response to our trickery made him go up a notch in everyone's estimation. For the most part he was as dedicated and serious about our mission as the rest of us. We needed a comic break every once in a while to relieve the monotony of the trip, but we all considered ourselves pioneers heading for unevangelized fields. We were going, not as tourists, but as servants.

When we docked at LeHavre we were instructed to get on the boat train to Paris. About the only other thing we were told was "don't drink the water, and watch out for the women." Besides our suitcases and cameras, Lyall had his accordion and I had a typewriter. In total, innocent ignorance we got on the train without first purchasing a "billet." When I tried to pay the conductor with a Canadian ten-dollar bill, he sneered at the funny-looking purple bill as if we had just printed it.

For a while we thought we would be thrown off the train, but the conductor and his superior seemed to conclude that we weren't smart enough to be pulling a con game, so they let us ride on.

Our problems were just beginning.

We arrived in Paris and discovered we had missed the train we were supposed to take to our assignment in Beziers in the south of France. Poor ol' Lyall looked at me, because I was the guy who was supposed to know what he was doing, and I didn't know beans.

We knew there were others from YFC meeting at L'Hotel de la Madelaine, but we had no address. I explained our predicament to a fellow at the American Express window and he suggested we get a taxi.

"But I don't have any French money for a taxi."

"Get the driver to take you to an Exchange, and have him wait for you."

That sounded good, so we found a taxi and I told him, *"Le Terminus, s'il vous plait, pour changer le cheques du voyageur,* you wait, *et je vous payez."* Boy, that's lousy grammar, but that's about what I said to him.

Ah, oui! Oui!"

I guess we weren't the first green birds just off the boat. So off we went. The two of us sitting in the back seat of the taxi with no money, and we don't even know where the guy is taking us. We finally got some money changed, and then the cabbie dropped us off at L'Hotel de la Madelaine, and charged us most of the currency we had just gotten.

Lyall stayed with the bags while I went in to register. *"Non. Non, monsieur. Ce n'est pas vrai."* We were in the wrong place. Evidently there was another hotel with a similar name. I went outside and there sat Lyall on his accordion case looking pale and bug-eyed. I glanced up and down the street and realized we must be right in the center of one of the worst red light districts in Paris.

We found a cabbie who assured us he knew where we wanted to go, and we got in. He gave us the grand tour of Paris, and we just sat back there with our eyes bugging. We didn't know what was coming off. Finally he turned down this dark, narrow side street. We didn't know if he was planning to rob us or what.

I got out and looked around the dingy street and said to Lyall in English, "I don't think this could be the place."

A head came over the balcony upstairs and a voice called, "If you are looking for the Youth For Christ headquarters, this is it!" I could have kissed him!

Ken Welch had already arrived. We rested a day and then boarded the coal-burning *"vapeur"* train headed south. We pulled out of the station at 7 A.M. and the 400-mile trip took until 8 P.M. The only way to cool off was to open the windows, but then the black soot blew in on us. By the middle of the day it was so hot we didn't care how dirty we got, so we arrived in Beziers looking like three black-faced minstrels.

We were met by Jean Schaffner, a middle-aged man with rather pointed features who was pastor of a small Free Church. Schaffner, who was to serve as the interpreter during our tour, explained that we were to be billeted in the palatial home of a local wine merchant. That sounded good, but they put all three of us in one room with two beds. We were so tired from the trip that we were staggering, so we pushed the beds together and crawled in. I don't even remember who slept in the crack.

Any veneer of glamour associated with gospel globetrotting was already wearing thin, and we hadn't even started yet. Getting to know the Schaffners was a treat, though. They had lost all their possessions during the war, and were living quite modestly. They had not lost their sense of humor or their dedication to Christ, and they welcomed our help in trying to spread the gospel throughout the area. Madame Schaffner, a rather matronly woman, ruled the roost in the home and was very solicitous of us. But the three teens, Suzie, Jean Mark, and Mimi, were a bit shy.

Our first campaign was held there in Beziers in the town hall. The crowds turned out from the first night; about 45 percent of the congregation were young people. People brought their dogs along and sat there and smoked and chatted among themselves, which was very distracting.

Ken did an excellent job working through an interpreter. He would give a short phrase, then pause and wait while it was translated, then another phrase. Despite the distractions, some people were converted. There was one man who sat right on the edge of his chair so he could hear better. The last night of the two-week crusade, hands started going up, indicating they wanted to be saved even before I started singing.

The poor accommodations, questionable food, extreme heat, and all the other inconveniences suddenly didn't matter any more. It was such a thrill to see that the gospel could triumph over all the limitations, all the barriers. We were far from being career missionaries. We had had very little preparation, and didn't even speak the language. And in spite of all that, God could still use our feeble attempts to bring people to himself.

Our next campaign was in Sete, about twenty miles south and right on the seacoast. The auditorium we were to use was littered with bottles from a dance that had been held there, and was generally filthy. We cleaned up as best we could and started passing out handbills and hanging posters announcing the meetings. The populace didn't seem overjoyed at our being there, but by the end of the week we had 100 or so attending the meetings, with twenty-nine decisions.

Our missionary journey continued on through Narbonne, Agde, and Pezenas. Basically we did the same thing over in each city, and yet certain events, certain people became etched in my memory. For one thing, there was the constant awareness of the limited time we had to serve. So we pushed ourselves to make the most of each day.

Bastille Day, July 14, was impressive because for the first time in at least 100 years the gospel was preached in an open air meeting in Beziers. Four or five hundred people came and listened attentively to the hour-and-ten-minute program. Many made decisions, and many more exhibited a hunger for the literature we were giving out.

There was a big burly fellow who sat chain-smoking during a meeting in Sete. When the noise of the crowd disturbed him, he told everyone to shut up. He returned the last night of the crusade, and at the end of the meeting raised his hand for prayer.

Pezenas proved to be a very difficult place. The first meeting there was a fair turnout. The second, only a few showed up. The third and last meeting, only one lady and her dog were there. We held services anyway, and at the close of the meeting that woman accepted Christ as Savior. The next week she became a member of the church Jean Schaffner pastored in Beziers.

There was the priest who attended every night in Agde, presumably to check out what we were saying. The mayor who cooperated, and the one who didn't. The Communist newspapers and propaganda displayed throughout the region. The spreading fig tree we ate under in the courtyard of our quarters. And the digestive problems that plagued us.

All my life I had been exposed to missions and missionaries at Wortley Church, yet I was unprepared for the experience of being on the field. Now I had smelled the smells, tasted the tastes, wiped off the dirt, and walked down the streets, tiptoeing over the sewage. I'd seen Jean Schaffner and his family existing on so little, yet serving the forty or fifty souls who comprised their little church. It was not popular to be a believer in France, but in spite of that they were seeking to serve the Lord and win others. Compared to them, the comfortable Christians in North America seemed complacent, self-satisfied, and content. I had gone to France thinking I could be a blessing to those people. Instead, they were a blessing to my life.

Our last week in Europe was spent at the Youth For Christ Brussels Conference in Belgium. We were there in time to witness history unfolding, for Leopold was deposed as king. There was a minor holy war with Communists marching and Catholics running into the cathedrals with their arms filled with flowers. The city was in an uproar, but the conference went on in spite of it all. I met some great people that week, and got some fabulous photos, but quite frankly I was ready to chuck it all. I wanted to get home.

To make it back to Ontario in time for the opening of school, I had booked passage on a chartered flight. To my utter dismay I was informed that because war had broken out in Korea, the United States government had commandeered all chartered flights and there were people stranded all over Europe. After a week of running around, trying desperately to get some kind of a flight across the Atlantic, I was finally booked to fly out of Luxemburg on a Seaboard and Western DC-4.

I took a train to Luxemburg and then was told, "I don't think I'll be able to put you on that airplane."

"Now just a minute," I snarled, and I lit into him. I'd had all the run-around I could take. After some discussion I realized he was holding out for an extra twenty dollars under the table. In desperation I peeled off the second to last of my travelers' checks and signed it over to him. Then I got out to the runway and discovered the inside starboard engine had broken down. We stood around for hours waiting for them to repair it, so they could test the plane.

When we were finally allowed to board, guess where my seat was? The window next to that starboard engine. "Lord, I don't know about this. I hope she makes it." Our first stop was Iceland. We deplaned at 4 A.M. and I spotted a Trans-Canada Airlines plane adorned with the most beautiful maple leaf I had ever seen. I'd never thought of myself as an overly sentimental patriot, but that emblem of my country sure looked good.

Another nine-hour flight over water brought us to Gander, Newfoundland. I prayed for that engine the whole way. During our two-hour layover in Gander, I noticed a Canadian *Newsweek* magazine with the smiling face of an All-Star pitcher I knew. The closer I got to home, the more I realized just how homesick I had been.

From Gander we flew to New York. From New York to Montreal. By this time I'd been in transit so long I wasn't sure what day it was. I knew it had been a mighty long time since I'd had a bath and a bed. I didn't have any money left for a hotel, so I just had to keep going, and I boarded a red-eye flight to Toronto. I got to the long barracks-type building that served Toronto as an air terminal by 4 A.M. My mind was numb, but I knew that my wife and daughter were waiting for me at the Keswick Conference Grounds near Bracebridge, Ontario.

With my last travelers' check I bought a bus ticket to Bracebridge about 100 miles due north. Then a cab to the conference grounds. It was hard to believe I had once thought it glamorous to be a world traveler.

I was informed my family was in a cabin back in the woods. I took off with more steam than seemed humanly possible after that trip. I found the cabin and pounded on the door.

"Oh, it's Barry!" I heard Butch exclaim, and she flew into my arms. Boy, did she feel good. We couldn't even think of anything to say. We just hugged each other.

"Where's the baby?" I finally asked.

"She's asleep."

"Can I see her?"

"Sure."

We tiptoed in to our little sleeping princess. She'd grown,

and her hair looked so much thicker. Most of all she looked so beautiful. I picked her up and said, "Derry Dane, this is Da Da." She blinked her eyes groggily and I gave her a kiss and put her back into her crib. She went back to sleep, and I went back to hugging my wife. "Sweetie, I really missed you. I'll never go away for that long again."

SIX
NOBODY KICKS
A DEAD HORSE

The inspiration I received from my European jaunt, coupled with enthusiasm generated at a Youth For Christ Directors' conference in Chicago, had me flying high. The young people involved in YFC in London seemed more than eager to soar with me. Attendance kept growing, and more and more of the kids were willing to participate.

The first and third Saturdays of each month were our showpieces when we would bring in outside speakers, such as Bob Pierce, Redd Harper, Stuart Hamblen, Torrey Johnson, Dr. H. H. Savage, and Bob Cook—all the big wheels in YFCI. These would draw the big crowds of young people and the adults who supported the work financially.

Alternate Saturdays we would have small rallies, or rallies in outlying areas, or every once in a while just a fun night. I wanted to get the young people involved and give them outlets to serve the Lord, so I developed a group of talented kids to take part in the various meetings. We had a quartet, a trio, a trumpet trio, a pianist, an organist, a male vocalist, a female vocalist, and a girls' trio. They came from various churches. I would take turns dragging them with me all over southwestern Ontario.

The big problem was that often it seemed as if I were supposed to be in three places at once. It wasn't unusual for me to quit work at 4 P.M. on a Friday, pick up whatever group was going to help me that weekend, and arrive home on Sunday night. Somewhere I got the brilliant idea of turning to the students of the London Bible Institute for help in some of these projects. Out of that student body came leaders such as Roy Lawson, Clarence Shelly, Murray Hicks, Stan Walker, Dave Bell, and Doug Routledge. Since they were students, and mostly from out of town, they were not all available at any one time, but they all pitched in and helped.

We developed a board of knowledgeable men who were willing to work as well as give leadership. They tried to keep reins on me when I came up with too many "impossible" ideas, but they had the spiritual courage to try most of them. One of the most important was the desire to give the young people a concern for world missions. They responded beautifully, and soon the rally was sending regular support to the Schaffners to help establish a church in Agde, France.

As director, it seemed I directed the cast, the finances, the janitor—everything. YFC had become a full-time job, yet I was still holding down my full-time teaching position, and I couldn't be slipshod about that. Not only did teaching pay for our bread and butter—it was my career, my calling, my security. Since my European venture had precluded summer school, I was still taking night courses at the university and I had to keep up my grade average. I wanted that degree, for it meant that I would one day be in line for a principalship. As long as I was part of the educational establishment, our future was secure. Besides, I enjoyed teaching.

When I had been transferred to Princess Elizabeth, I tried a new tact with the discipline bit. I lugged the hockey game my father had made for me when I was in high school from his basement to my classroom. This was no ordinary homemade affair, for my father was a craftsman. He had taken an eight-by-four-foot sheet of three-quarter-inch plywood and transformed it into a rink, with three-inch sides to keep the puck from careening off the board. He had painted it to make it realistic, with lines and all. The nets were shaped like threes lying on their sides, just like the pros. The fittings were of brass, the netting of curtain material.

To play the game, an ordinary washer was used as a puck, and you slid your second fingers into little figures that represented players. One hand played goal keeper and with the other one you shot goals. I kept the board waxed so slick that the little puck would ricochet all over the place. It was really fun.

So instead of punishing a kid for not doing his work on time, I would use the hockey game as an incentive. If you finished your work, you got a turn at playing hockey, as long as you didn't disrupt the class by hollering. They really loved that game, and would work hard to earn the privilege of playing.

With my work schedule, university classes, and YFC, I didn't get to spend much time with my girls. What spare time I did have, Butch and I used to make plans for building a home on our lot on Langarth Street. By acting as my own contractor, and doing any of the work I could myself, I figured we could squeeze by financially. We would have a living room, dining room, kitchen, three bedrooms, bath, and a full basement. We figured that would take care of all our needs as our family increased in the future.

In spite of the hectic schedule I made for myself that year, there was always a nagging feeling in the back of my mind that I wasn't doing enough—that there was something else I should be doing. Perhaps that's why I pushed myself so hard.

The musical Palermo Brothers had just returned from their third trip to Italy and really sparked the opening night of our World Vision Rally at Beal Tech auditorium. The crowds grew each night. Sunday evening when Bob Cook spoke, we filled the 1500-seat Capitol Theatre and put 600 more in the Victoria Theatre around the corner where we had set up loudspeakers. Between the size of the crowd, and having the head honcho sitting on the platform, I was really revved up and I led the singing rather athletically, with the perspiration running freely.

Afterward Bob said to me, "Man, whatever you do, you give it your best, don't you?"

"For the Lord, Bob, you are right," I exclaimed, and then hoped I hadn't sounded too pious. But I meant it.

"Well, anyone who is as gung ho as you are is going to get his share of criticism, so I want to give you one bit of wisdom. Just remember, nobody ever kicks a dead horse."

I had occasion to remember those words many times. I guess I have to admit I have kind of a sledge-hammer personality. Coming on strong can turn some people on, while it turns others off. Perhaps that's why the Lord gave me such solid men as board members to keep my feet on the ground.

During the summer of 1951 I concentrated on getting our home built. First I got Dengate on the horn. "Hey, Duffy, how about helping me chop down a tree?"

"I've never cut down a tree."

"Neither have I, but we can do it. We've got to get it down so the bulldozer can get in there. I've seen my father do it. It looks easy."

"What kind of a tree is it?"

"A huge old horse chestnut. I hate to cut it down, but it's right where my living room is going to be."

Neither of us knew what we were doing, but I climbed up the tree and proceeded to trim off some of the branches. We were so clumsy and were making such a mess, we got to laughing until I literally rolled out of the tree. Fortunately I wasn't too high at the time and wasn't hurt. It was just so exciting to be actually started on our home after planning for so long.

Two big events happened that fall. First, after six years of part-time study, I received my B.A. degree from the University of Western Ontario. I was nearly twenty-six years old and was glad to be through as a student. Then we moved into our home, our very own love nest. It was good to be back on Langarth Street. It's difficult to explain the sense of continuity it gave me to be back in the old neighborhood. I had come back to the scenes of my childhood—to my roots.

One very special part of living there was that Kerry Jane would have an opportunity to know my parents better. I loved to see my father take my two-year-old daughter by the hand and go for a walk down the block, just as we used to do when I was a boy. He'd take her tiny hand in his strong one and match his steps to her little legs. I could see him pointing this way and that and could almost hear him saying, "See those pretty red flowers? Those are salvias. And see how the trees make an archway over the street? Look, Kerry Jane. That lady across the street is waving at you. That's Mrs. Mare. Wave back."

Yes, it was good to be back on Langarth Street.

The next challenge that came down the pike from YFCI headquarters concerned the Fifth Congress of World Evangelism sponsored by Youth For Christ, which was scheduled to be held in Belfast, Ireland, in August. Naturally this was billed as the "biggest yet," and the powers that be wanted as many local YFC directors to attend as possible. The minute that brochure hit my desk I wanted to go. Perhaps because my dad had always talked about Ireland so much, I had always had it in my heart that I wanted to go to Belfast.

Then the thought hit me, "If I raise the wherewithall to go to Ireland, for just a little more I could hop over to France and retrace my first missionary journey, just as Paul had done." The more I thought about that the more feasible it seemed. That would give me an opportunity to visit the Schaffners and see firsthand the little church our rally was helping support. This would mean I'd have to leave Audrey and Kerry Jane for about a month, but at least it wouldn't be all summer as the first trip had been.

I was so convinced that this was of the Lord that I did something out of character. I committed myself to going even though I hadn't raised all the capital before the deadline. I had no idea where the extra funds would come from, or how I could leave with any less than I had budgeted, yet I felt confirmed in my heart that I was to go.

The day before my scheduled departure I busied myself with a few household chores so they wouldn't be left to Audrey. I was standing on a ladder cleaning out the eaves in front of the house when the phone rang. I climbed down and entered the front door in time to catch it. A familiar voice said, "Hi, Barry. I'm concerned about your trip to

Europe. Do you have all your money yet?"

"Matter of fact, I'm $165 short."

"Well, you have it now. I've been led of the Lord to give it to you."

That was a real stimulant to my faith! I had been running around beating the bushes to do all I could to raise that money myself. Then when there was no time for me to do anything more, the Lord provided the means for me to leave with all the bills cared for.

With a big lump in my throat, I left Butch and our curly-headed doll and flew to the south of France. The reunion with the Schaffners was heartwarming. Jean was extremely grateful for the motorcycle that London YFC had provided for him, since this enabled him to reach more people. We revisited the stops of the first trip and met with some of the converts. Most thrilling was the report that the lady, who (with her black dog) had been the only one to attend the third meeting in Pezenas, had not only been converted, but had started selling Bibles and New Testaments. To date she had sold about 300 of them at her place of employment, in the bus, or wherever she had an opportunity. She had become a missionary in her own right.

On Sunday I preached in the little converted store building that served as a meeting place for the church in Agde. I said something to the effect that this was a demonstration of the power of God, who could even convert a shoe shop. They loved it.

This was my first experience preaching with an interpreter, so I mimicked Ken Welch by saying just a short phrase at a time, then waiting while Jean translated. After awhile, a sort of pattern, a rhythm developed and I found it wasn't as difficult as I had imagined.

Touring with Jean Schaffner was a humbling experience. He was so dedicated to the people he served, yet he had an impossible task. His family existed on a pittance. His clothes were so threadbare that I gave him one of my shirts before I left. He looked all choked up and said, "Barry, this is the first white shirt I have had since before the war."

I was touched to notice that he was wearing the "new" shirt when he took me to the train station. As the iron monster pulled away I leaned out the window to wave good-bye to him. My mind was gripped by the sight of him, as if some photo cells in my head snapped a picture that was to remain indelibly imprinted in my brain. Here was this humble servant of God wearing a second-hand shirt and strings in his shoes for laces, smiling, bidding me farewell. If the Holy Spirit has ever spoken to me, he did so at that moment. As the train rounded a curve that was to take Jean out of sight, I heard a voice asking, "What right have you to leave him here all alone and go back to that comfortable, lucrative teaching position?"

"Lord, I have no right. No right at all," was all I could answer.

I set foot on the "Old Sod," for the first time filled with mixed emotions. Should I be here if I belonged back in France? Belfast was being inundated with the Bob Cooks and Bob Pierces of YFC. What use would *I* be? I was just a rookie from London, Ontario.

As if to calm my doubts, I was given an opportunity to participate in the meetings that were going on all over the city. John Wesley White was preaching in Wellington Hall and he asked me to give a report on France. Then I was asked to lead the singing in the Great Victoria Street Baptist Church, where revival was breaking out as I'd never seen it. People were going to church all over the place, and they kept opening more churches to accommodate the crowds. While I was emceeing the meeting one night, the pastor came to me and said, "Listen, Moore, there is a car coming for you. You are going to the Sandy Row Methodist Church to preach. And brother, you'd better preach!"

Talk about shaking in your boots! I got to Sandy Row and the building was packed. I mean packed to capacity! And here I was a green kid who didn't know from nothing, and I got up there and preached. But God blessed, and several people were saved that night.

If God was using me like that, he couldn't possibly want

me as a missionary in France, could he? It didn't seem logical. Surely he would give me a clearer indication of his will if that was what he wanted.

The final meeting of the Belfast Congress was held in Windsor Park Stadium, with over 35,000 people in attendance. At the close of the meeting a call went out for Christian workers to go down under the stands to deal with those who had come forward. In the confusion afterwards I bumped into a ruddy-complexioned, square-jawed, Irishman. "Sorry, buddy, I didn't mean to knock you over," I apologized, holding out my hand. "My name is Barry Moore."

"Barry Moore!" he repeated with a strange look on his face. Then he returned my smile, took my hand, and slapped me on the back. "Moore, you're not going to believe this, but I was just sitting out front in that mass of humanity wondering how I could find you."

"You-you were wanting to find me?"

"Yes. Evon Hedley has been telling me about you. I'm Bob Munn and I'm a missionary in France, teaching at the European Bible Institute near Paris. I've been hearing about the work you've done in France. Why don't you come permanently?"

Wow! Here I was back at square one. Did God want me in France? We walked back to my hotel and talked. Munn had such an effervescent personality that he became an instant friend. I felt I could confide in him and we talked on and on through the night, literally. Dawn was just breaking when he mumbled, "Barry, this is the second night I have had practically no sleep."

"Who wants to sleep nights like this when God is working in men's hearts and lives?" I countered. I was really wound up. "Why, this move of the Spirit in Belfast could influence the whole world for Christ."

That "chance" meeting and the recurring vision of Schaffner waving good-bye greatly affected me. When I got home Butch could tell something was bothering me. "Do you really feel God is calling you to be a missionary?" she asked.

"I'm not sure. I have responsibilities here. I've signed a

contract to teach school this year. There's this new house to pay for and my family to support. Besides, there's all the work to be done for Youth For Christ here."

I threw myself into pushing YFC as never before. Perhaps I was trying to wear myself into a frazzle so I'd be too tired at night to be haunted by the vision of an overworked French pastor waving at me. Yet God kept blessing our efforts in London and the work continued to grow. So much so that I had a surprise visitor in my classroom one day.

The minute I spied Dr. Don Sutton I knew why he was there. Dr. Sutton was an inspector for the school board, who had taught me grade seven and also a biology course at the university. I knew him quite well, and under ordinary circumstances would have been glad to see him, but class inspections were always scheduled ahead of time. This unorthodox appearance could only mean that there had been complaints and he was trying to catch me unprepared.

"Good afternoon, sir. How are you?"

"Fine. How are you?"

"OK. What's up?"

"Oh, I've just come to observe. Just thought I'd like to see how things are going."

"Are there any fears that they aren't going well?"

"No, no. Go ahead as usual."

I carried on as if he weren't sitting back there, then after dismissing the class I asked, "This is a little unusual, isn't it?"

"I didn't want to say anything ahead of time, but I'm here at the request of your principal."

"For what?"

"Well, Barry, there is fear that all the religious work you are doing might be getting in the way of your teaching."

"Doc, you know me. I couldn't let my teaching slip. That would be unchristian."

"I realize that, and frankly I'm not concerned. You are an excellent teacher, and were well prepared. You'll get top grades on my report."

Thinking it over later, I really got to feeling I was being

persecuted for my faith. The very idea of a sneak inspection! After considering the situation more thoroughly, I realized why the principal might suspect me of being slovenly in the classroom. YFC was getting lots of publicity for all its activities and rallies, as well as the area rallies. I presume Dr. Sutton had just read my name in the paper so often that he got suspicious. That really bothered me. I didn't want my outside activities to be a stumblingblock to anyone, but at the same time I had all kinds of ideas about other areas of service that Youth For Christ could and should be involved in. The time had come to admit I wasn't a superman.

"Look, fellows," I explained to the board of directors, "this job has just gotten too big to be handled on a part-time basis." I then laid out the entire program and just how many man hours each effort entailed. "We are now at the point where the work is either going to progress or regress. Treading water just doesn't work, so we're going to have to find a full-time man to take over these responsibilities."

"Well, where are we going to get a man who could do all that?" one of the men asked.

Fred Hinton leaned across the table, looked me straight in the eye, and said, "Thou art the man!"

"Aw, you're crazy," I replied. But deep in my heart there was a sneaking suspicion that perhaps I "wert" the man.

The entire board was adamant that I take the position. The most I would concede was that I'd pray about it. After all, that would be a big step. Here I was earning five thousand dollars annually, with an automatic six-hundred dollars to be added because I had gotten my degree, and YFC could offer sixty-five dollars a week tops. And then I'd have to raise the money from supporters.

After the report the inspector had turned in, I'd been offered a spot teaching high school for the next year. I was on my way up! I felt certain I could one day be a principal and then perhaps go into administration or superintendency in the public school system. As an educator I had status, guaranteed secure income, a pension plan, all the accoutrements. What would I have as a full-time YFC director?

This wasn't the kind of a decision to be made overnight, and I wrestled with it for weeks. Was I going to teach or preach? Finally I got out of bed one night, went into the living room of our little bungalow, and pulled out a note-book. Across the top of the page I wrote "pro" and "con," and drew a line down the middle. Under "con" I wrote *money*. Then I sat there and stared at the page. Financial security was the only real negative I could come up with.

When I had first mentioned it to Audrey all she had said was, "Are you sure you want to leave the teaching profession?" I knew I could count on my wife being on my side no matter what I decided. My family had cautioned, "Be careful," but that was all. I'm sure my in-laws weren't thrilled with the idea, but they hadn't made any strenuous objections. There were just no more "cons," and yet I was still hesitant.

Finally I prayed, "Lord, I'm not trying to make a deal with you, but I want to ask for two things. If I am to go full time, please give me a sense of confidence that you will do this for me. First I have to have assurance for my own kids, not just for Kerry Jane but also for any children we may have in the future. I just cannot go and preach to other people's kids if my own are running hell-bent to destruction, depreciating your name.

"Then Lord, I'd ask that you would keep us out of debt. We will do our best to live within our means. We aren't asking for luxury. I just don't want to dishonor your name by owing any man."

I slipped back into bed, and as I was telling Audrey about my prayer, I had absolute peace that the Lord would grant my two requests. "Let's do it," I exclaimed.

"OK," she replied, as assured as I was that the Lord would grant my petitions.

Since I had signed a contract with the school board for the 1952-53 session, I felt duty-bound to finish out the rest of the school year. With that understanding I made my commitment to the YFC board.

There was one board member I was concerned about. I'd first met Jack Fickling when I spoke at a Christmas party for the young people of the Salvation Army. Jack was a sharp-witted character and we hit it off right away. Butch and his wife Shirley were yakking away and discovered that I was the little pest who used to sit behind Shirley in grade school and pull her hair.

The Ficklings had been in charge of the young people's fellowship for their citadel, and by the time the evening was over I was convinced Jack would be a natural for the YFC board. We were outside walking toward our cars with a cold wind whipping around us when I broached the subject. "Jack, you should come on our board, and be a representative for the Salvation Army. Would you consider that?"

"I'll let you know."

"Well, let's get together about it."

We did just that, and the offshoot was that he came on the board in January of 1953 and began helping Fred Hinton with the ushers. Since then I'd had some doubts about him. He was a great guy, and we got along well, but some of his statements made me wonder if he'd ever really had an experience with the Lord. Here he was on the board of London's YFC, on my recommendation, and I wasn't sure he was a Christian!

The only thing I knew to do was take the bull by the horns and talk to him about it. Early in March we drove to Toronto together to see the Maple Leafs play. All the way home I was trying to think of a diplomatic way to bring up the subject of his salvation. I didn't want to insult him. I didn't want to lose a friend. Yet I had to talk with him.

We got all the way home and he pulled up under the streetlamp across from our house on Langarth Street before I worked up the nerve to ask, "Jack, do you mind if I ask you a question?"

"What is it?"

"How do you know you are saved?"

"Well, I don't do this or that or the other thing," he rambled on.

"Jack, do you expect to get to heaven by what you don't

do? I don't want to embarrass you, but. . . ."

"You're not embarrassing me. If I don't want to listen, I'll tell you to mind your own business."

"Well, do you really know that you have trusted Christ? Would you like me to show you how you can really know?" I reached into my shirt pocket for my New Testament and began sharing the plan of salvation.

He not only listened, but there in his car he accepted the Lord as his Savior as we prayed together. Instead of losing a friend, I not only won a soul for the Lord, but our friendship blossomed.

As spring began its budding, I drew up my resignation and took it to the superintendent, Dr. G. A. Wheable. The "Chief," as we called him, was a fine fellow with a Methodist background, and he had real spiritual perception. After handing him my resignation I stayed and chatted with him a bit.

"You know, Barry, I admire you for what you want to do for the Lord, but I think I'll just hold this resignation for a while. If you have any second thoughts, if you reconsider and change your mind in the next few days, just give me a call."

"I won't be calling you, Chief," I blurted out. "I know this looks like a dumb move, but I'm very confident of it."

"Very well, but if you should ever decide you would like to come back, I'll have a job here for you until you are thirty-five."

His words were rather like a pat on the back from the Lord, reassuring me that God would take care of me. I walked out of that office knowing I was turning my back on that phase of my life, and anticipating what was to come.

Top: Redd Harper with me and Muriel Barrie, YFC secretary.
Bottom: Counseling at YFC headquarters with Larry (left) and George.

SEVEN
WHEREVER
HE LEADS

Adapting to my new life style was easier than I had expected. The pressures involved in a full-time youth ministry were not new to me, and I felt natural and at ease with all the related activities. It was not unusual for me to return home about 10 or 10:30 at night too tense and excited by the meeting I had just attended to think of going to sleep. My pregnant wife would be snoozing away, while I was wanting someone to help me unwind. More often than not I'd put in a call to Jack Fickling, one of the few people I knew who would respond to an invitation at that time of night.

"Hello," he'd answer in his gravelly voice.

"Hey, Flicker. What are you doing?"

"Talking to you."

"Don't be smart with me! Why don't you come on over and have a little fellowship?"

There would be a pause on the line while he talked to his wife, then, "Be right there."

Our "fellowship" sessions were held in my basement, where I had set up my hockey game after I'd resigned from Princess Elizabeth School. After the problems and tensions of the day, it was the perfect way for me to relax and have fun at the same time. We were never satisfied with one game, but would play the best two out of three. Then four out of five. Or five out of seven. And on and on. For a night cap we'd play a game or two of darts.

After a day spent in my dingy office on the corner of Carling and Talbot, talking on the phone, counseling kids who dropped by, making plans for our next "biggest ever" rally, and an evening fund-raising event in a nearby church, I needed the diversion.

Part of the pressure of the job was the continuing need of coming up with new talent for a big rally every other week. We had a string of ex-movie people, ex-athletes, and even an ex-con or two. We brought in a pro-football star once and that ended up in a pie-throwing contest. The whole idea was to make the teenagers have a good time, let them relax and feel at home, and then hit them with a spiritual punch.

All the rallies were growing and soon the board recognized that I needed some assistance, so they hired a Bible student, Dave Bell, to help out part time. He was to have responsibility for the counseling, followup, and juvenile delinquency work, as well as the rally at Port Burwell.

Bell was at our house one day discussing some of the ideas I had for future advances. "Always shoot for the moon," I told him. "And I guarantee you will hit something higher than the trees."

He kind of shook his head, turned to Butch, and sighed. "You absolutely amaze me, Audrey. How do you put up with this guy?"

"Easy," she laughed. "He's away most of the time. We get along fine."

I hoped she was teasing. It was true that I was gone a good deal of the time, but I was determined that I was going to be around for the birth of our second child. That proved to be easier said than done.

As the due date approached I arranged my schedule so I wouldn't be too far out of town for any length of time. The date arrived, but the offspring didn't. That baby was due, and due, and due. No action. This seemed more frustrating to me than to Audrey. After all, she wasn't going to miss out on anything.

The whole staff was scheduled for a meeting in Hanover,

Ontario, nearly one hundred miles north of London. "Are you sure you'll be all right?" I asked before I left.

"Sure, sure. Go ahead."

"I'll call you when I get there," I promised, and I did.

"Nothing stirring," she reported.

"OK, fine. I'll call you the minute the meeting is over."

While the others were eating sandwiches and cake, I put in another call. "No, I've been resting pretty well. I'm just uncomfortable."

"I'll call again as soon as I get to the city, before I drop off all the kids."

It was nearly 1 A.M. before we got back to London and my call was answered by a groggy-sounding voice. "Nothing yet. Go ahead and take the kids home."

It took about an hour to take all the young people stuffed into our new station wagon to their homes and then get home myself. I crawled into the sack and was out like a light. Then about an hour or so later I heard Audrey up.

"You'd better get dressed. I think it is time."

"You gotta be kidding," I moaned.

That night I learned to appreciate what a woman goes through to deliver a child. I was glad I was there to offer what comfort I could, because she had a rough time. When I was informed that Barry Mark weighed in at ten pounds twelve and one half ounces, I understood why. They kept Audrey in recovery for quite some time, but they rolled this baby over in a little cart. He looked like a fullback. His coloring and features were similar to his sister's. My son!

Having Mark around didn't change my schedule much. I was on the go as much as ever. He did put a slight crimp on the hockey sessions Jack and I had in the basement, though. More than one night we'd get carried away with our enthusiasm and we'd be whooping and hollering downstairs only to have the basement door open and a perturbed mother call out, "I hope you're satisfied!"

Slam!

Then we'd realize it was 1:30 A.M. and the wailing upstairs let us know we had been a bit loud. Shamefaced, we'd finish our game.

Audrey really did put up with a lot from me. For the most part she was a very dutiful, obedient wife. There was one time, though . . .

I came home from a series of meetings and asked how the talent contest I had set up for the London rally had gone.

"Oh, just fine," she giggled, with a mischievous grin.

"Really?" I asked, my suspicions aroused.

"Yes. We had a lot of real talent and everyone seemed to enjoy it."

"Who won?"

"Kerry Jane."

"What!"

"Well, you know she sings all those little songs from listening to the children's records when she is falling asleep. She practiced with the pianist and sang 'Open up your heart and let the sunshine in' and never missed a beat. There were others in the contest with more talent, but she was so cute that everyone applauded the most for her. So she won."

"You know I would never have allowed you to enter her if I'd been home."

"Yeah, I know," she grinned. She looked more pleased and proud than repentant. It was obvious there was nothing I could do.

"Well, we had said that the winner of the contest would appear at the big rally this Saturday, so I guess there is nothing we can do but have her sing. Do you think she will perform in that huge auditorium with hundreds and hundreds of people staring at her?"

"She'll love it," Butch predicted.

The advertising for the rally promised "One of the most attractive soloists who has ever appeared in London Youth For Christ." I used the same phrase in introducing her and added, "Ladies and gentlemen, would you welcome Kerry Jane Moore." Out she sauntered in a frilly pink organdy dress, her long blonde curls bouncing in rhythm with her steps. The crowd ooooohed and aaaaahed.

I bent down with the microphone and asked, "How are you, Kerry Jane?"

90

"Fine."

"Are you glad to be here?"

"Yes."

"Are you scared?"

"No."

"Why aren't you scared?"

She just looked at me and gave me a big smile, and the crowd melted. The pianist started her introduction; she sang like a pro and brought the house down. Canadians are a bit conservative and don't usually applaud at functions like YFC rallies, but they did that night. As she was walking off the stage she half turned and waved at me, and they applauded all the more. Nothing like being upstaged by your own daughter!

Even though I hadn't planned it, Kerry Jane's performance had proved to be a crowd pleaser, and it was a lot of fun for me, too. The one thing that really bothered me about all my frantic activity with YFC was not having enough time to spend with my family. I did have a lot of help, though, and never had to travel around by myself. Perhaps because of my early involvement in team sports, I always thought of myself as a team person. When I traveled I would always have one of the high school groups, or some of the LBI students, the Volunteer Quartet, or some of my board members with me. If I was just going to some little rinky-dink place that didn't generate much enthusiasm, or if the students all had conflicts, I could always count on Fickling to go with me.

Jack had been through the thick of World War II, and maybe because I missed it, I was enthralled by the stories of his exploits. If he got tired of telling them I'd say, "Come on, Flicker. Tell me a couple more stories and I'll sing for you." For some reason he liked hearing me sing, so I'd practice my solos, and I'd get some interesting illustrations for sermons from him.

"One thing I don't understand about you, Barry," he mused one night as we were driving toward London.

"What's that?"

"Well, I've been with you in places like Guelph where you preached the commencement exercises and got a standing ovation, and I've been with you in little meetings like tonight where there were not more than a dozen young people there, and you preach just the same no matter the size of the group. I'd think you would tone it down a bit when you just have a handful of kids."

"Well, Flicker, that's the only way I know how to do it. In sports you give 100 percent for every game, and that's the same thing I do when I'm preaching. How can you give a half-hearted invitation to accept Christ?"

"Seems to me you make it hard for someone to say yes."

"I guess I do, but that's just because I want to make sure the person means it. There were three times in my life when I made decisions for Christ, and I'm not really sure which time I was saved, because it wasn't clear to me exactly what I was deciding—what was expected of me, and what God would do for me on the basis of my repenting and turning to him. That's why I try to make it clear when I'm preaching."

"Hmmmmmm," was his only comment.

Perhaps the hardest meetings to pull off were the "Fun Nights." Instead of bringing in talent from the YFCI circuit, I'd have to come up with something new, different, exciting, and fun. It couldn't come off as being silly, yet the program really had to move. We reached a lot of kids in those meetings who would never have come to hear anyone preach.

We'd do things like having an Olympic Party. This was held in the basement of a church with a couple hundred people attending. I'd planned it all out. We'd divide into two teams, the Pyromaniacs and the Kleptomaniacs. To start the event off with a bang, I'd prevailed on good ol' Harry McKenzie to run in with a candle representing a torch so he could hand it to me as the symbolic gesture that would initiate the "Olympic" games.

Bless his heart, Harry had been sick in bed with the flu for three or four days, but he got up, dressed in his shorts and sneakers and snow shoes and grabbed a cab over to the church even though it was five degrees Fahrenheit that night. He was burning up with fever, but determined to be dependable until the end—which didn't seem far off.

Well, he came staggering in, knobby knees and all, stumbled down the steps and across the floor, handed me the "torch" and collapsed on the floor. We carried him out and put him in a cab. The audience thought it was all part of the fun and they just howled.

We then proceeded with the games, such as discus throwing—to see how far you could throw a paper plate, and things like that. When the Pyromaniacs won an event, they would sing their theme song—"Keep the Home Fires Burning." The Kleptomaniacs would sing "Steal Away." It was exhausting, but a lot of fun.

All these gimmicks had a purpose. They put young people into a more receptive mood. At the close of the evening I'd give a five-or ten-minute talk, and tell them that if any of them wanted to know how to become a Christian, to come see me afterwards. That was hard-sell again, I guess, but a number of kids were saved as a result of those nights.

Ever since my first trip to France I had kept in contact with Jean Schaffner and the rallies had continued to support his work. His regular reports, and visits by Bob Munn when he was in Canada, kept the cause of missions before the kids and me, too. Any time I'd see Munn or get a letter from him, he'd always ask, "When are you coming back?"

After three years of this, coupled with the continual nagging of my conscience, I decided it was time for me to make another trip. This time I'd be the preacher, so I needed to find myself a versatile musician to accompany me. Clarence Shelly came to mind immediately. Shelly had first strolled into my office wearing a plaid shirt and reminding me of a guy who had just finished milking the cows. He was a real live farm boy who loved the Lord and was studying at the London Bible College. Incongruently, he was also a pianist, and could play the organ, cornet, and vibraharp. As a student, he would have the summer free, so I put it to him: "Let's go. We have the contacts and it will be all set up for us," I assured him.

With his enthusiastic agreement I wrote Schaffner, who immediately began planning on that end. With the blessing of the YFC board, I began booking "deputation" meetings in my spare time to raise the necessary funds. The Volunteer Quartet as well as musical groups from the rallies really extended themselves in helping in that effort.

After a big farewell at the airport, Clarence and I flew off for Europe, ready to conquer southern France for Christ. Before I knew it, I was sitting in a hotel room in Sete, France, looking at my ticket. After all the meetings raising money, being away from my family night after night, it suddenly hit me that I wasn't going to see them again for three months.

I felt a little nauseated and it hurt to breathe as I fought to control my emotions. I had just arrived and I was more homesick than I'd ever been in my life. It was all I could do to keep from running back to the airport and returning home. My little wife and adorable children were half a world away from me and I missed them so much I felt physically ill. The only solution was to throw myself into the work so hard that the long summer that stretched before me would soon pass.

We held our meetings in four towns, pitching our tent in the most conspicuous place available to us. Schaffner would interpret my simple gospel messages, and the people came. They came and they listened and many responded.

In one town the Communist mayor allowed us to use the central plaza gratis, but nuns with wide-winged chapeaux stood at the stairs leading up to the plaza and warned the people not to attend. The closest we ever came to a riot was when a gang of ruffians tried to frighten us away. They started slamming down the heavy steel rollaway grills used to burglar-proof the stores. Over and over. Bam, bam, bam. The noise was disturbing, but we continued in spite of it.

The sweat, dirt, and hostility of the semi-atheistic culture disillusioned us with the prevailing religion of the region, but the evident spiritual hunger challenged us. One evening as we were driving back to our quarters, Shelly and I got to talking. "Just think, Clarence. If we can reach as many people as we have in just a summer, what could we do if we were here full time?"

"I have been thinking about just that," he acknowledged.

"Schaffner says I could be preaching in French in a few months if I worked on it. We could do evangelistic work in a community until there was a nucleus of believers to start a new church. After securing a regular pastor for them we could go on to a new location. We could do that all across France. Then I could bring my family over here to be with me."

"Sounds exciting, but what do you think Audrey would say about that idea?"

"I don't know. Maybe I'm just dreaming out loud."

The conversation ended with no definite conclusions being drawn, but the dream lingered on.

When September arrived I was torn between wanting to continue the work that God was blessing, and hurrying home to my loved ones. Telling the Schaffners good-bye was difficult, but I think they had an inkling that we might be meeting again one day.

Being home was a blessing I appreciated more for having been gone so long. Our little house on Langarth Street, that Audrey had worked so hard to turn into a home, seemed luxurious compared to the living accommodations in France. All the little creature comforts I had always taken for granted now took on a different meaning as I considered leaving them to serve the Lord abroad.

Kerry Jane was cuter than ever, and doing so well in school. She reminded me of Butch in many ways, and was just a joy to be around.

Markie was nearly two, and turning into a real kid. He looked very much like his sister, but had an entirely different personality. He was into everything. Always exploring. Investigating. When Kerry Jane was his age I could tell her, "No-no. Don't do that," and she would stop. I'd do the same with Mark and he would give me a mischievous grin and his black eyes would twinkle at me as if to say, "You've got to be kidding."

Was it fair for me to consider taking these youngsters away from their homeland? Would uprooting them be traumatic? And what about their grandparents? All four of them doted on these two precious children and spoiled them a bit. What would they say about a persistent dream that kept drawing me back to France?

What about Audrey? She had been with me all the way when I had left teaching to go full-time with YFC, and although there had been times when our finances were very shaky, she had never complained. But selling our home and furniture, and leaving our families and friends? That would be asking a lot.

When I finally brought up the subject, she said, "Oh, that's what's been bothering you."

"You mean you'd be willing to go to France as a missionary?"

"It would be better than staying at home without you."

"It would mean I'd have to go back to school to get some theological training, and the only way we could swing that would be to sell our house and furniture."

Her round brown eyes got a little misty and her lower lip quivered slightly, but she replied, "If that's what the Lord wants us to do, then I'm willing."

What a sweetheart!

EIGHT
GETTING THE PUCK
IN THE NET

"Barry, I never expected you to stay with YFC London for very long," Dick Dengate commented when I told the board of my intention of going to France as a missionary.

"You didn't?" I questioned, feeling a little put down.

"No, I really didn't. I felt from the very first that you were too big a man to stay here. It seemed to me that God had a bigger plan for you and this was just a stepping stone to a higher calling."

"Well, I appreciate that, Duffy," I replied, feeling quite nonplussed.

With the approval and blessings of that group of men in whom I had great confidence, I tendered my resignation, effective June 30, 1956.

My next decision would be where to go to school for further training. A call came from Bob Munn who was about to return to France. "Have you considered Columbia Bible College in South Carolina?" he asked.

"Never heard of it."

"Well, there are a number of excellent Christian liberal arts colleges, but you already have that background. If you just want Bible, then I'd suggest you look into Columbia."

With that recommendation, I put in a call to South Carolina and talked to the director of admissions, John Ker Munro.

"I'm just about to leave on a vacation," he explained, sounding rather in a hurry. "This is quite a coincidence, though. I'm going to be visiting some friends in Byron, Ontario, on the outskirts of London. Why don't we sit down and talk while I'm up there?"

I felt a "coincidence" as wild as that just had to be of the Lord, so naturally I made plans to meet with Munro in a few days. We sat under the shade of the maple trees in the spacious yard of the suburban home and discussed my situation. The more I heard of Columbia, the more I realized that the degree of Master of Biblical Education and Missions they offered was exactly what I needed.

Feeling very confident of the Lord's leadership in this decision, we put our house up for sale. Finding a buyer without too much difficulty seemed another affirmation that we were indeed following the Lord's plan for our lives, so we began selling our possessions.

We had lived in our love nest for five years, and we both had saved for years before we were married to buy our furniture and appliances. I know it was tough on Butch to watch people cart away some of her prized possessions, but she took it like a trooper.

The day we were to leave we were down to some lawn chairs we'd borrowed from my folks. Jack and Shirley Fickling came over to say good-bye, as did my folks and Audrey's. Her father acted as if the world had come to an end. My dad wept on my shoulder. Flicker blubbered worse than either of them. And the women really carried on! I'm not easily moved to tears, but when we pulled away from Langarth Street I was bawling like a baby. I make no apologies for that. We were turning our backs on all that had been dear to our lives, and it was tough. We weren't running capriciously after some distant rainbow, but felt assured we were following God's leadership. Still, I'd be a liar if I said it was easy.

As we headed out Highway 401 toward Detroit, Kerry Jane continued to sob as if her little heart was broken. Mark didn't really understand, but our little girl just cried and cried. In trying to console her, Audrey finally discovered the problem. In her little mind she had figured that because her grandparents were old, they would surely be dead before she returned and she would never see them again. After we had reassured her that we would be back at Christmastime for a visit and she could see them all then, she calmed down.

Looking back, it seems the Lord provided for our needs in an exceedingly gracious manner. When we pulled into Columbia, South Carolina, for the first time we really felt like aliens. But because of an amazing "coincidence" we were not friendless. The Munros had invited us to stay with them until we could find housing. More than just needing a roof over our heads, we were in need of a home away from home in a loving, family-like atmosphere. And that is just what they granted us. Their home was rather small, and they had four boys ranging from six to fifteen. But they squeezed us in and never for a minute let us feel we were imposing. Even more important, after we found a house on McArthur Avenue a couple of weeks later, we were still allowed free run of their home. John didn't have a hockey game in his basement, but he did have a ping-pong table in his garage, and he would shed the dignified air he had around school and play and laugh with me until near midnight.

The housing we had found was, well—*adequate* would be a kind description. It was a shell with no foundation or basement. Not the kind of a house necessary in Canada. Then too, there were the creepy, crawly visitors that drove my wife up the wall. We just weren't used to them.

After starting out our marriage with brand new furniture, we were now sitting on chairs and sleeping in beds that had been used by countless people before us. Our circumstances were not optimum, but we were determined to adjust. It was tough being a student again at thirty, but this would be our home for the next two years and we consciously tried to look for the best in the situation.

We enjoyed the warm winter and found our neighbors to be extremely friendly. Kerry Jane adapted well to her new school and soon had little friends running around the house. Best of all, for the first time since our marriage, I was home a good deal of the time. We didn't have funds to pay for entertainment, and didn't know many people to visit. So we just kidded each other about how homesick we were and enjoyed being together.

We became close friends with a young couple who lived across the way from us, Ken and Carolyn Barber. When we were first moving in, Ken presented himself at our door offering to help. How could anyone resist an offer like that? His lovely young wife was in a very advanced state of pregnancy, but she sat and chatted, smiled and encouraged the rest of us during the unpacking.

About a week later, on the day their firstborn was due, Ken drove off with Carolyn to the hospital. Audrey was so excited and happy for them, you'd have thought we'd been friends for years. I was sitting at my desk near our bedroom window when Ken's car pulled into the lane between our houses. "Well, what's the good word?" I called out to him.

"The baby was born dead," he replied, and went into his house. That really shook me up. I went and told Audrey, we talked about it a while, and then I tried to return to my studies. There was no way I could concentrate when I knew Kenny was hurting so badly. I picked up my Bible and went over to see if there was some way I could console him.

"Want to talk?" I asked when he answered my knock.

"Sure. C'mon in."

"You know, Ken, in the Bible it tells about how King David had an infant son who died, but David had confidence that he would see the boy again someday. Would you like to know how you could have that same assurance?"

"Yes, I would."

I opened the Scriptures to him, and he opened his heart to the Savior. He later shared with Carolyn and she was converted also. The adoption of a newborn eased their pain some and they were extremely thankful for the little one they were given to love.

Seeing Barber growing in the Lord was a source of real joy to me, and I delighted in sharing with him some of the truths I was learning in class. For the first time in my life I was really digging in and studying the Bible and I loved it. Because of my teaching background I was able to pick up a little extra cash by grading papers and serving as a teacher's assistant, but my main job for two years was to feast on the Word of God, and I devoured it voraciously.

That first year George Duncan, pastor of The Tron Church in Glasgow, Scotland, came for the "Deeper Life" conference at Columbia. I was enamored with his accent, his messages, and his use of alliteration. After the services I went to him and asked how he managed to do this.

"Well, I'll tell you," he expounded magnanimously. "First you analyze the text. Then you crystalize the truth. Finally, you humanize the teaching."

I latched onto that little gem, and put it to immediate use. Discovering that homiletics was merely a theological term for the principles of pedagogy I had learned in teachers' college encouraged me. Maybe I hadn't been doing too bad a job in my preaching. The main blow to my ego came when I realized I had never really understood repentance, and had left it out of my preaching.

Because of this, a determination grew in my soul that I was going to distill the theological truths I was being taught to the point that the smallest mind could comprehend them. If I was going to be involved in pioneer missions, presenting the way of salvation to people who had never heard it before, I wanted to be able to make it as clear as possible.

I'm sure that some of my professors thought I was being pesky, but I'd ask again and again, "What exactly is repentance?" "What does it mean to be born again?" "What is conversion?" I polished the answers with the same professionalism that a hockey player would use in perfecting his slap shot. If I had but one opportunity to explain to a person how to have a new life in Christ, I wanted to be sure to get the puck into the net.

Then there was this required course on prayer. I wondered how anyone could teach a whole course about praying, but the Rev. Frank Sells opened my eyes. First he insisted we develop a prayer list. He even suggested that if the Lord allowed us to win someone to Christ, we were obligated to pray for that new convert in the name of conservation of results. That really hit me, for I couldn't even name all the people who had made decisions in the countless YFC meetings I'd held in the past decade. I vowed to discipline myself in the future in this matter of prayer, and I began a daily list.

I had returned to school to get more knowledge of the Bible, but more than that, I was introduced to the deeper spiritual life, to a more disciplined prayer life, the sovereignty of God and the lordship of Christ. All this was a further confirmation that we were in God's will.

Everything was coming up roses. Our biggest problem was trying to keep Markie out of the swamp. When we had first moved into the house on McArthur we were warned that the marshy bog across from our place was full of alligators and snakes. Rattlesnakes! We were pretty green when it came to things like swamps, and it might not have been as bad as we envisioned, but we were certain it was no place for a not-yet-three-year-old boy to play. So it was put off limits. Well, for an exploratory-type kid like Mark, that was just a challenge.

One day I looked out the window, and here comes this little figure clad in a dark brown snowsuit, coming up from the swamp. "Mark! Get in here," I yelled out the door. He came trudging over. "Son, you know you are not supposed to go in that swamp."

"I wasn't in the swamp, Daddy," he protested with the first lie I'd ever caught him in.

"Mark, I just saw you coming out of the swamp."

"Oh, no, Daddy. I wasn't in the swamp."

"I saw you!"

"No. I wasn't in the swamp," he persisted, as an old echo sounded in my brain, *"That's three."* He looked so cute and innocent, but I felt that for his own protection I had to administer corporal punishment so that he would never go in there again.

I learned that the old saying about a spanking hurting the parent more than the kid had a lot of truth in it. Kerry Jane had always been so eager to please us that it was difficult to understand Mark's defiance. He was such a persistent kid. Stubborn. So much like his old man that there was bound to be a clashing of wills. I tried to explain to him that I loved him very much, but that he had to obey.

The holidays spent at home, as well as visits by my parents, helped our first year at Columbia to fly by very quickly. That summer the four of us crowded into one bedroom at the Snelgroves' home. When fall approached and it was time to return to South Carolina, the farewell scene was so different from the year before. We were looking forward to returning to our house, friends, and schoolwork.

A trip to the Greater Europe Mission headquarters in Chicago in December of 1957 rang the old year out in a positive way, for Audrey and I were officially accepted at that time by their board. Along with Clarence Shelly and nineteen other candidates, Dr. Warren Filkin, Dr. Carl Armerding, Sr., and the Rev. Noel Lyons, formally welcomed us into their fold. On the completion of my schooling and raising of funds, we were to begin a church-planting, evangelistic ministry in France.

For my master's thesis I chose to do a critical study of YFC titled "Youth For Christ: Yesterday, Today—and Tomorrow?" That was an arduous task, and I don't know if I could have made it without Butch. She encouraged me, listened to me think out my ideas, and then typed the copy on our little clickety-clack portable typewriter.

I was wallowing deep in theological thought one day when Ken Barber strolled over and made a great pronouncement. "Mark's going to be a singer one day."

"What makes you say that?"

"Come listen."

I followed him out back, but even before we rounded the house so we could see the kids' swing, we could hear Mark singing at the top of his lungs, "Jesus loves me, this I know. . . ." The whole neighborhood could probably hear him. Chip off ye ol' block!

Since I didn't have to keep a strict schedule that spring, I was able to do quite a bit of speaking, which gave me a jump on my deputation work. I spoke in a number of churches in North and South Carolina, Georgia, and Oklahoma. When I was invited to speak for some big "do" at a YFC in Ontario, I decided to keep a promise I had made to Kerry Jane and had her fly home with me. That was her first flight, which was a thrill to her. It gave her an opportunity to visit with Granddad and Grandma Snelgrove, and I had my little girl all to myself for awhile. She was a delight.

As time for graduation drew near we became more and more conscious of the race we were going to have with the stork if we wanted our new addition to be born in Canada. The doctor had suggested at Christmastime that it would be best for Audrey to stay in Canada and not try making such a long trip so close to the time she was due in June, but she was determined she wanted to be with me. Besides, her babies were always late.

Commencement exercises were held June second. We started loading a trailer with our stuff that afternoon. A public health nurse, Ruth Ross, who lived in Woodstock, was going to travel with us. She came over, took one look at Butch, and shook her head. "You'll get halfway home and have a baby on your hands," she predicted.

"Aw, she'll be all right," I assured her. "It only takes a day and half to get there."

"And how long do you think it takes a baby to be born?"

I tried to act confident, but as we drove along I kept watching Butch out of the corner of my eye. She wiggled and squirmed, obviously uncomfortable, but she didn't complain. We stopped for the night, and nothing happened. Crossing the Canadian border we grinned at each other and let out a collective sigh.

Then after being so anxious to make it back to London, Timothy Lee didn't arrive until June thirtieth, weighing in at ten pounds and four ounces. We were a bit amazed to find we had produced a blond, blue-eyed son who looked very much like my sister Kathy. He also had a sweet disposition, and fit immediately into our family group.

With three children we had to find some kind of accommodations for the duration of our fund-raising for France. A contractor friend from Wortley Church was building a small subdivision east of town and he agreed that we could move in with an option to buy. Then at the end of the year he would take the house back.

So I moved my little family into 48 Arcadia Crescent, only to discover as it grew dark that the electricity didn't work. I didn't know what to do; we had to be able to see. We were still living out of boxes and couldn't find anything, so I went in search of help. No one had moved into the houses on either side of us, but I spied a guy up on the roof of number fifty-two fixing his TV antenna. I figured if he was smart enough to do that, maybe he could help me.

"Hey, you cotton picker," I yelled up in what I hoped was a friendly voice. "Do you know how to get the electricity on in my house?"

"I'll be right down," replied a voice from above.

I watched as this stockily built guy made his way down the ladder. "Hi, Barry, how are you doing?" he asked with a big grin, extending his hand.

"Fred McDonald! Well, this is great. I didn't know you lived here." Fred was a truck driver for the Canadian Pacific Railroad and used to deliver parcels to the YFC office in the Dixon Building. He was a most congenial character who would always ask if I was still praying for him. True to form, that was the first thing he wanted to know.

"Yes, I'm still praying for you," I assured him. He then followed me over to the house, and to my great chagrin discovered the reason the electricity didn't work was because I hadn't put any fuses in the box. I never claimed to be a handyman, but at least my ignorance was good for a hearty laugh.

A few days later Don and Shirley Balch moved into the house between the Moores and the McDonalds. Don had been converted in a "satellite" rally in the St. Mary's town hall back in 1955 when I was director of YFC. I remembered the night he came forward with his girl at his side. They were now married and members of Wortley. They were just the kind of people one would choose as neighbors. Don is as affable and dependable as a St. Bernard.

Having folks like the McDonalds and the Balches living nearby relieved my mind about having to hit the trail for a series of meetings and leaving Butch behind with three small children. I knew in case of an emergency she would have help available.

So the team of Moore and Shelly set out to raise money for a tent, a portable organ, and all the equipment we would need in our evangelistic efforts in France, plus our support. Clarence brought with him a new team member, his bride of two months, Pearl. Pearl was no stranger, for she had served as secretary of YFC and I knew she was a gifted organist.

Over the next few months we took over 300 meetings. It seemed strange that although we would get generous offerings for buying equipment, few pledges for support were made. It was greatly encouraging that many people accepted Christ in those meetings, for the gospel was always presented, as was the need in France.

It was an exhausting schedule, but most frustrating to me was the thought of Audrey staying home with those little kids by herself. When our itinerary brought us near London, and I returned home, I'd find all kinds of chores piled up. But I never had enough time. I'd do well to get the grass cut before it was time to leave again.

After the two years in Columbia when our family was together most of the time, it was especially hard to be separated. When we had a meeting in Kitchener, Ontario, I decided to take Mark along so I could spend a bit of time with him.

"How would you like to be my song leader tonight?" I asked him. He was excited by the prospect, so that night I stood him up on a stool and we had a four-and-a-half-year-old song leader. He waved both arms in time with the music as the congregation sang, "The Lord Knows the Way Through the Wilderness." Then he sat on the front pew like a little angel while I preached. I was so proud of him, but it was all the harder to leave him the next day.

We went to Belleville, Ontario, where we held twenty-nine deputational meetings in sixteen days. The next week we returned to Peterborough, Ontario, for a second crusade there. It seemed everywhere we went, invitations were extended for us to hold evangelistic crusades, which seemed an indication of our acceptance. But we were not yet getting the long term supporters we needed for our first term as missionaries.

Then I returned home to find a confusing letter from Greater Europe Mission headquarters. They had changed their minds and now wanted me to come and teach in the Bible School at Lamorlaye rather than do the evangelistic type work we had agreed upon. This really threw me for a loop. The Lord had so clearly led in all our decisions to this point, why this sudden change of direction?

I reread the letter. It seemed to be slamming a door in my face. But that just couldn't be. Butch and I had sold our house and furniture because God was leading us to a pioneer work of evangelism in Europe. I'd spent two years in school training for that work. The Shellys and I had raised $12,000 to buy our equipment. The door *couldn't* close now. It just couldn't.

NINE
THE BLESSINGS
OF GOD

"What would you say if I told you we might not be going to France?" I asked Audrey.

She laughed and said, "I'd say you were crazy! Everything is already in gear."

"I kid you not."

When she saw I was serious she looked from me to Clarence and Pearl. The Shellys and I had just returned from another series of meetings and I had already discussed my reservations with them. While she continued making dinner for us, I explained that the Shellys felt they should go to France no matter what role they were called upon to fill.

"I just don't have peace about this," I continued. "I've felt so confident about God's leadership in this thing, and we've been going across the country telling people this is what we are going to do, and now to be faced with switching roles makes me feel uncomfortable. I don't know what to do."

This dilemma tormented me. I prayed and prayed, but found no solution. My mind was in such a continual turmoil that I had to find some physical outlet to soothe my emotions. I'd go to the Fanshawe Golf Course and take out my frustrations on the little white pill. At night I'd take an old tennis ball and go down in the basement and throw it against the blank front wall. The *thunk, thunk, thunk* of that ball bouncing against the wall must have driven Butch crazy, but she didn't say anything.

It seemed so incomprehensible that God would throw me such a curve. He had led us clearly in our decisions during the past years, and now it seemed he had turned his back on us. Didn't he have a plan for my life? Wasn't he going to use me when I was available to him?

An invitation came for me to serve as president of Canadian Youth For Christ. I was flattered that they had considered me, but I hardly even prayed about the offer. That was a closed chapter in my life. I had to go forward. I had to do something, but what?

Here we were with three kids, living in this little house on the outskirts of town because of the good graces of a friend, using second-hand and borrowed furniture we had managed to scrounge up, with no idea of what would become of us. I'd given up my career as a teacher, then quit as director of YFC, sold our home and possessions, and now God was closing the door to France in our faces! It didn't seem fair. How could he do this to us? I felt a kinship with Jacob as I wrestled in prayer over what seemed an impossible situation.

Wortley Church and one lady friend of the family had continued to support us financially since the early days of YFC. This kept food on the table, but there was not a cent for extras. In our deputation meetings the Moore-Shelly team had received and accepted many invitations to return to do evangelistic campaigns. This meant my time was committed, even though I didn't know whether or not we were going to France.

I was conferring with a trusted friend about my situation when a call came from Belleville. "Hi, Barry, this is Jim Blackwood," the vaguely familiar voice rang out. Blackwood was the director of YFC in Belleville, but I didn't know him well.

"How are you doing, Jim?" I asked.

"Fine. Look, you made quite an impression when you

110

were speaking in various churches here, and now I'd like to arrange a city-wide crusade for you. I'll organize the whole thing, line up a song leader and singer, take care of all the details."

An offer like that coming out of nowhere took me by surprise, but my mind latched on to it immediately. In the hundreds of meetings we'd held in the past months, I'd done all the booking, made travel arrangements, found housing, emceed the meetings, led the singing, taken up the offerings, and even sang solos and trios with the Shellys before beginning my sermon.

"You mean all I'd have to do is preach?" I sighed.

"Right. I'll handle everything else."

"Best offer I've had all day," I laughed, and the agreement was made.

Having all that pressure taken off me, I could concentrate on my sermons. I polished up some that I considered my best, with the snappiest titles. "'Squares' in the Family Circle," "The Asbestos Kids," "A Night in an Eastern Ballroom," and "What's in a Kiss?" Getting up to preach without having responsibility for all the preliminary events gave me much more freedom in my delivery.

Blackwood had lined up Wes Aarum to lead the music for the crusade, and I welcomed the opportunity to get to know him better. Wes was involved in YFC and I'd known him casually for a number of years. He was not only a superb pianist and a great platform man, but an excellent preacher in his own right.

"I've got a problem," he confided to me one night while we were having a late supper after the meeting. "There is an elderly gentleman in Tillsonburg who recently found the Lord, and now has a great burden for his hometown. Mr. Greer has graciously offered to pay all the expenses involved in having an evangelistic crusade in Cabri, Saskatchewan, so his former friends and neighbors might hear the gospel."

"So what's the problem?"

"Well, the crusade is set for October. He asked me to go, but I have a conflict. Now that you're a big-shot city-wide

111

evangelist, why don't you go?" he teased. "I could make all the arrangements for you."

"Well, I don't have anything else scheduled for October," I admitted. "I guess I could."

Then I confided to Wes my predicament about going to France. Matter of fact, I'd discuss it with anyone who would listen. People must have gotten tired of that monologue, but it weighed so heavily on my heart that I had to get it out. I had given my word that I was going to France, and I'd always been the kind of guy that if I said I was going to do a thing, I did it. I believed in keeping my word, and yet I did not have peace about going and teaching at that Bible school.

We had good results in the Belleville meeting, as we did in a number of other meetings that summer in spite of the fact that I was having this personal crisis. Finally I made an appointment to talk to my pastor. Martin Wedge had been at Wortley since 1956 and the church was growing under his dynamic leadership, so I had a good deal of confidence in him.

The towering, gray-haired minister listened to me patiently for some time, then said, "Let's look at this objectively, Barry. What's happening to you now?"

"Well, different people have told me, 'If you don't go to France, we'd like to have you come and conduct a crusade.' I don't know whether God wants me to go into evangelism here. I feel very strongly that God wants me in France, and yet every cotton-picking time I get up to preach, people are saved."

"Barry, do you think that the devil is opening the doors for you to have evangelistic meetings on the Canadian scene?"

That statement hit me. It was just like in a cartoon strip when a light bulb turns on to indicate an idea dawning. "Of course not!" I exclaimed.

"Barry," he counseled firmly, "God has set before you an open door, and no man can shut it. So if the door is open, go through it."

And that was it. I'd never wanted to be an evangelist—

had neither sought nor desired a calling in that direction. But now it seemed so clear that this was what God had been training me for all those years. I could hardly wait to get home and tell my patient wife who had suffered with me through all the months of indecision.

"But if that is what God wanted all the time, then why did he let you think you should go to France?" she questioned.

"I've been thinking about that. If I had gone into evangelism directly from YFC, I'd never have gone to Columbia Bible College. I needed the grounding in the Word that I received there. My ministry will have much more depth because of my time there. Also, I can now give a challenge for missions to others with the knowledge that we were willing to go ourselves."

With this renewed assurance that God was really working in my life, I was running over with enthusiasm during the trip to Cabri, Saskatchewan. Mr. and Mrs. Greer drove Lyall Conlin and me in their sedan and I talked all the way. We arrived in the little farming community and Lyall and I were put up in the Cabri "Hilton." It featured one bathroom for the whole floor of rooms. The rest of the boarders were itinerant truckers, ditch diggers, and such, but Conlin and I didn't care. He seemed to have caught some of my enthusiasm, and it was good to be working with him again as we had done that summer in France.

The opening meeting was on Monday night, the eleventh of October—Canada's Thanksgiving Day. That was really bad timing, and to make matters worse it had poured down rain all day. The streets were not paved and had turned into a muddy, slimy mess the locals called "gumbo." We went over to the old town hall where the meeting was to be held, and it was so dirty and smelly it made you wonder what it had been used for the night before.

Lyall began playing the piano and I sat down to wait for the crowd to appear. First a Scandinavian-looking woman shuffled in. She had mud nearly to the ankles of her boots, her coat collar was turned up framing her face, and her knitted hat was pulled down over her eyebrows so that not much more than her nose was showing. A middle-aged couple entered. Then a couple of women who looked like sisters. The Lutheran pastor arrived. Then a couple with their young son. Counting the Greers, that was a grand total of eleven people. I'd been preaching to 800 and a thousand back in YFC. I couldn't help but moan, "Lord, are you sure you know what you are doing?"

I went over to Lyall and whispered, "We had bigger crowds than this in France." He just grinned and went into the introduction for the first hymn. I led the singing. He played a special on the accordion, and then we sang a duet. Because there were so few people there, I put the podium down off the platform and spoke from the floor. At the end of the sermon I felt it would be unwise to extend a public invitation, so I simply offered to give "spiritual assistance" to any who would be interested in coming to talk to me later.

The next night we had about fifteen people. The next night sixteen. It increased until the last Sunday afternoon there were eighty or ninety people in the hall. Considering the population of the town was only 720, that wasn't bad. This was the only time I asked for public commitments. "If you have made a first-time, new commitment to Jesus Christ as Lord during these meetings, would you please stand?"

Thirty-three people rose to their feet. I talked with them a bit, encouraging them in the things of the Lord. I got their names to add to my prayer list, then dismissed the meeting. Afterwards many of the people gathered around me and asked if I would return for another series of meetings. I told them, "If you want me to come back, write and extend an invitation."

On our way home we were to stop in Moose Jaw, about 150 miles down the road, so I could speak in the Alliance Church for the evening service. This was one of the largest Christian and Missionary Alliance churches on the prairies and was well known because of a Sunday night songfest that was aired on radio station CHAB.

We dragged in there over a half hour late. Lyall hurried to

the Hammond and began playing background music while I fought to get my muddy boots off without getting the muck all over myself. The young emcee covered over the delay masterfully, and I got up and apologized profusely for being late.

I only had about fifteen minutes before air time, so I gave a report on the blessings we had just witnessed in Cabri. At exactly 9:00 P.M., the songleader took over. "This is Harvey Schroeder welcoming you to CHAB, Moose Jaw." He then turned and led the choir in a rousing rendition of "We're Marching to Zion." I sat back and observed as Schroeder handled the choir, led the congregational singing, sang a solo, and read the requests that had been mailed in. Smooth. Exceptionally smooth for a guy who couldn't be more than twenty-five or twenty-six.

After the program I apologized to him personally for being late and leaving him holding the bag. "Oh, that's OK," he cracked. "We just sang four verses of every hymn in the book." He introduced me to his tiny, redheaded wife, Ella Mae, and their little daughter Karen, and we all talked a bit. "Would it be all right if I called you sometime?" I asked him.

"Yeah, sure," he responded, but I found out later he had just accepted the position of music director for the Alliance church in Edmonton, Alberta, and wouldn't be able to take any time for at least the next year. I tucked his name back in a nook of my brain, though.

I was all excited when I got home, and anticipating the next crusade in January. This was another fill-in for Wes Aarum, but I didn't mind. God had used me in Cabri; surely he could do the same in Regina at the Scarth Street Apostolic Mission. I'd never heard of an "Apostolic" church, but my reservations were quickly dismissed as I fellowshiped with the pastor, E. L. McCrae. He was as excited about winning souls as I was. And we were having a fine meeting, when, about Wednesday or Thursday, the telephone rang and a voice asked, "Is this Brother Barry Moore?"

"Guilty."

"Well, I'm the Rev. Robert Lardon from the Apostolic Assembly in Swift Current. Brother, I hear you are having the blessings of God."

"Well, we're having good meetings, if that's what you mean."

"Yes, and God has urged me to call and invite you to come to our church for a similar meeting."

"Well, thank you very much. When?"

"Next week."

"Oh, but, I've already been away for a week, and my wife is home with our three little kids . . . ."

"Brother, you pray about this and talk to Brother McCrae."

The minute he mentioned McCrae's name, something clicked. I whirled around and said, "You sicked him on me, didn't you?"

"Would I do a thing like that?" he grinned.

"Yeah, I think you would. What would my wife say about this?"

"Well, Brother, just pick up the phone and call your little lady and see."

I put in a call to Audrey and the first thing she said was, "Who is this fellow, McCrae?"

"He's the pastor here. Why?"

"I just received a dozen red roses from that church in appreciation to me for letting you go do the crusade."

I really appreciated that delicate touch—letting my wife know she was important and acknowledging her part in my ministry. "What shall I do about those other meetings?"

"Well, what can I say?" she giggled. "When will you be home?"

I told her I would be home in another week, but while I was on my way home from Swift Current I stopped over in Regina to do a YFC meeting on Saturday night. I put in a call to an old friend of mine, Rev. Dick Simpson, who had pastored in London, but now had a church in Moose Jaw.

"Good to hear from you, Barry. Where are you?"

"I'm in Regina. Gonna do a YFC rally tonight."

"Where are you going to be next week?"

"Oh, I'm going home to Mama."

"Oh, no, you aren't! I have an evangelistic crusade all

promoted and prepared, and my speaker has taken ill and can't come. God has just now told me that you're to be our evangelist."

"Well, God hasn't told me that."

"You just call Audrey and tell her that God told me to tell you to come, and see what she says."

So I put in another call to my sweetheart. "Audrey?" was all I said, but something in the tone of my voice must have given me away, because she wailed, "Oh, no! Not again?"

Talk about doors opening! I finally got home after that Moose Jaw crusade with invitations to five more meetings, and I found a letter waiting for me from Cabri. It was signed by thirty of the people who had just made decisions, plus many others, and they were inviting me to come speak in the new town hall that was being put up.

Gleefully I went to share my blessings with Pastor Wedge. "Pastor, you must have been right. Here I am with no experience, and I'm a bit of a dummy anyway, but God is opening doors for me all over the place."

"Well, then, I think you need to share this with the church."

"What?"

"They've been supporting you all this time because you told them you were going to France as a missionary. Now that you are going into evangelism in this country you should tell them."

That was a tough proposition. Wortley Church had always been very mission-minded, and I had felt that these people I had known my whole life were proud of me for being a mission volunteer. What were they going to say when they heard I was going back on the commitment I had made?

The next Sunday evening I got up and stood near the communion table and I bared my soul to the church. After explaining all that had happened, I added, "Many of you have given donations to buy equipment for the evangelistic work in France. I'm going to be sending out a letter to all donors offering to return their money, but suggesting it be turned over to the Greater Europe Mission for use in evangelism in France.

Left to right:
At a kids' meeting on a Saturday morning—Regina, Nov. 1960.

Conlin, Moore, and Schroeder—Weyburn, May 1962.

Dad Moore.

The whole Moore family.

"Finally I want to ask you to pray for Audrey and me as we wait upon the Lord to open doors of opportunity for us. While on deputation this past year and a half, over 500 souls have been won for Christ. Many of these have been in small communities that have never had an evangelistic crusade. With the help of your monthly support, I've been able to go to these places that couldn't afford to bring in a high-priced evangelistic team. Somehow, I'd like to continue doing this, for his glory."

After the services, seven or eight people came to me and said, "It's all right, Barry. We didn't really think you were going to France anyway."

It seems they knew something I didn't. Jim Blackwood said practically the same thing. When the local YFC board had asked me for suggestions for a new director, Jim's name was on my list. He had been a success in the business world before going into Youth For Christ full time, and I knew him to be an efficient promoter. It was shortly after he had moved to London that he told me, "Aw, you're not a missionary. I think of you as an evangelist." Then he looked me straight in the eye and said, "I'd love to push your ministry across Canada." And that statement clicked.

"That's something to pray about," I mused. "I'm not the world's best businessman, but I know I need to set up some kind of an organization and incorporate or something. I should have a board of directors, and there will be all kinds of bookkeeping to do if the ministry is to be run like a faith mission.

"If you really mean that, Jimmy, I want to set up some appointments for us to talk this over with some men of spiritual insight. I'd like to get as much input about this as I can before we commit ourselves to it."

"I mean what I say," he replied. And I took him at his word. With Blackwood carrying the pressure of the details on his broad shoulders, I felt confident that God would bless this new ministry he was opening for me.

In between my out-of-town crusades, we got together with Jack Fickling at a fish and chip place for lunch one day. Another time we talked with Elliott Stedelbauer at the office of his car dealership. We discussed the possibility with pastors Bill Newell and Bill Sifft. We got advice from as many people as we could, and best of all we received encouragement from our wives.

I was determined about one thing. If I was going to continue spending so much time on the road, I couldn't leave Audrey and the kids out in the boonies in that little house. We sold that house for enough profit to come up with the down payment on a split-entry, three-bedroom home on the south side of London, about two miles from Wortley's new building. It had a family room as well as a large office for me, lined with bookshelves.

Then, after months of consulting with leading pastors, lay leaders, and Christian businessmen, the first board meeting of what was to be called Crusade Evangelism of Canada was held on Tuesday, August 30, 1960. There was such a meeting of the minds and oneness of purpose during that meeting in Toronto, that I had to feel this was of the Lord.

We agreed on a statement of faith as well as the policies and aims of the organization. After spending nearly two years in limbo, it was fantastic how our plans just seemed to fall into place. It was exciting, but at the same time very humbling to realize that the Lord did have a plan for my life, in spite of the times I had doubted it.

Looking back, I could realize that Audrey and I had been put through a time of testing, but for a purpose. The Lord had called on us to demonstrate our obedience, loyalty, and love. Now, after proving that we really put him above home or possession, family, friends, or financial security, he was ready to bless. I use the "we" purposefully, for with a wife less devoted to God and to me, I could never have arrived at this pivotal point in my ministry. We had been through the fire together, and it had drawn us closer to each other and to the Lord.

Blackwood and I had drafted an outline of campaign procedures to precede each campaign. He planned to begin laying the groundwork four to six months in advance of a campaign, setting up committees to involve local leadership. Although I admired his efficiency, the thing I appreciated most about Jim was that he realized all the organizing in the world could not bring revival. In the very first news bulletin we got out, he wrote a column emphasizing that the greatest prerequisite to the blessing of God on our meetings was prayer.

We then extended an invitation to Lyall Conlin to be the music master of the team. He had all the qualifications: He was a talented, dedicated musician who had proven himself a trooper, who could take the pace of an evangelistic tour, and could put up with spending so much time with me. As closely knit as we had become on the crusades we had done together, it was obvious to me that to work so closely demanded a special kind of friendship and loyalty.

Conlin had recently married Colleen Gurney. We didn't have to worry about Colleen understanding, for she had worked as my secretary while I was directing YFC. I knew her to be dependable and loyal, and considered her an asset.

All we needed to round out the team was a songleader-soloist. There were lots of possibilities for this position, but I felt that until we were certain a man was God's choice, it would be better to book different singers for a while.

Then Lyall and I set out for a month of campaigns in Saskatchewan. These had already been set up, but it seemed somehow fitting that the very first series of meetings held under the Crusade Evangelism banner was back in Cabri. Before we left I called Mr. Greer, to check in with the old fellow and report what God had been doing in my life.

"I don't think I can go with you this time," he responded in his shaky voice. "I ain't been doin' too good."

"Well, I'll be sure and give you a report when we get home."

"I'll pray for you," he pledged. That meant a lot to me because I knew he really would.

We returned to the prairie town to find the new town hall had been completed and the whole atmosphere was different. The crowds started at about 100 and went up to 150 or 175, with 300 to 400 different people attending, and a good response to the messages.

After Kindersly and a city-wide campaign in Moose Jaw, we returned home and I called to keep my promise to Mr.

Greer, only to learn he had just died. I stood beside Mrs. Greer at the funeral home, looking down into the casket at the face of the old man who had had such a burden for his hometown. "It was a good meeting," I assured her, "and the people who found the Lord the first time were all there."

"I regret that he couldn't go with you this time. But seeing him lying there now, I'm just so glad that he not only heard what God said to him, but he did what God told him to do."

I felt that was quite a testimony. I only hope the same can be said of me when I'm gone.

Our next big thrust was a two-week, city-wide campaign in the "Queen City"—Regina, Saskatchewan. This had been planned and promoted more than anything we had done to date. Herb Bock, a local pastor, was the crusade chairman. I had met him briefly when I'd spoken at the Art Museum the year before. His quiet, mild manner hadn't particularly impressed me at that first meeting, but in the days of planning for the crusade, he proved himself to be a master at handling detail, with a real gift for getting people to work together. Like an old firehorse, I was chomping at the bit, anxious for that meeting to begin.

Then the phone call came. "It's my brother," John Ker Munro explained. "He's in deep distress of body, mind, and spirit. He asked our sister to either get me or Barry Moore to come talk to him. I'm over a thousand miles from there, or I would go myself, because he really needs the Lord. Do you think you could drive up to Wiarton to talk to him?"

This was just one day before we were scheduled to fly out of Toronto for the Regina Crusade. It seemed evident that God had given his endorsement to our evangelistic efforts and I was loaded for bear. I couldn't wait for the meetings to begin, but after all the Munros had meant to me and my family, how could I tell John Ker no?

I picked up a baby-sitter, and Butch and I drove the 150 miles to try to win this man to Christ. We arrived at about one in the morning and the sister answered the door. We walked in and Ken was lying on the bed, drunker than a hoot owl. "It's Barry Moore, Ken," I shouted at him.

"Aw, sure."

"Look, I've driven over one hundred miles, and it's taken me three hours to get here. What do you want?"

"I shink I'd better trusht the Lord," he hickuped.

"Garbage!" I responded, and I lit into him. He was too drunk to understand subtleties, and I was too short on time and patience to pussyfoot with him. I let him know he was a sinner, and if he wanted forgiveness, he'd have to repent.

"I want shou to pray fer me," he declared. "Ah'm sherious this time."

"You'd better be," I warned him, and I got down on my knees and began to pray.

Despite his assurances that he meant business and was serious about a commitment to the Lord, I went to bed feeling very skeptical.

After too few hours of sleep Butch and I returned to London where I had to pack and prepare for the trip to Regina the next day. Since this was to be a big deal, Blackwood was going along. To save a few bucks we drove from London and picked up Conlin in Brantford on the way to Toronto. If everything had gone perfectly, we would have made our plane. But it was pouring down rain and the traffic was all snarled up. We missed our flight by two minutes.

Then I proceeded to browbeat myself. I'd cut it too short. I never should have wasted time going to Wiarton. That guy was drunk and probably didn't even remember me being there. And now we were going to be late getting to Regina.

The next flight in wouldn't arrive until after the service had begun. We hopped on board, praying that we'd get there in time for me to preach. At 8:30 P.M. we were still circling at 30,000 feet and there I sat, hotshot evangelist, chewing my nails, not able to do a thing. We finally landed and were driven to the meeting, but Wes Aarum had filled in and was just about to finish his sermon. We stood in the wings and watched as the invitation was extended and those responding came forward.

After making my apologies to the crowd, and closing the

meeting in prayer, I asked the local director, Herb Bock, for a report.

"We had 660 people here. We kept expecting you to arrive, so we dragged out the preliminaries for an hour. Homer James sang an extra solo, and Wes had the congregation sing four verses of every song. We stalled until a message came from the airport that there was an additional delay. Then I leaned over to Wes and asked him, 'Are you prepared to preach?' He leafed through his Bible and came upon an outline he must have used before. You saw the results."

"So you got along fine without me?" I asked, feeling deflated.

"Yes, and an interesting thing. Before you were ever invited for the meeting, the committee had discussed what evangelist to invite, and a number of them seemed to think we had to have Billy Graham, but your friend Doc McCrae reminded us that, "We really don't need a big name? God can speak through anybody.' I guess, despite the anxiety we felt for a while, God proved the validity of that statement tonight."

Then I really felt deflated. I guess it's good for all of us to be reminded once in a while that we aren't indispensable. I felt more dependent on the Holy Spirit than ever after that, and we had a fabulous meeting. We moved to the Exhibition Auditorium for the weekends. The 2,200-seat building was comfortably filled the first weekend, and it overflowed the second. Best of all, we had about 400 decisions.

An interesting sidelight: Three months after the crusade I got a letter from Ken Munro saying, "I never knew a dry time could be such a high time." He had really been converted. Six months later, he died of a heart attack.

While setting up some future crusades, I thought of Harvey Schroeder, and decided to give him that call I'd mentioned a year before.

"How ya doing?" I asked after identifying myself. "And how is Little Red?"

"Little . . . . Oh, Ella Mae. She's fine. We have a new son since we met you. Darrell. How's the crusading business?"

We batted the breeze awhile; then I invited him to come along for one of our meetings. He agreed to a trip to Nipawin, Saskatchewan, in February of 1961. Now, anyone who agrees to a booking in a place like that in the dead of winter is either crazy or he really loves the Lord. I was banking on it being the latter.

It's hard to describe what happened when the two of us began working together. We just clicked. People talk about marriages that were made in heaven. Well, Harv and I sensed a bit of that kind of magic in our teamwork. This guy was not only excellent with untrained choirs, teaching them by rote—he was a natural as an emcee, and he could put over a solo with the best of them. Besides that, he could take my teasing and give it right back to me.

When Lyall and I climbed into Schroeder's car for the trip south to Regina to get a plane, I was more than a little skeptical about starting out. The snow was so deep it was scraping the bottom of the car and you couldn't even see the sides of the road. We passed some cars in ditches, but that didn't discourage him in the least. "Schroeder, the only things making it on the highway are the big transport trucks. Don't you think we should wait until this is over?"

"Aw, Barry, don't sweat the small stuff." He grinned, pushing on.

I figured anyone who would fight a blinding snowstorm like that was game for anything, so I began to give him a pitch about coming on as a regular member of the team. "It won't be easy," I told him right up front. "You'll have to raise your own money, just like a missionary. You'll eat what they give you and sleep where they put you. There will be some big crusades, but we have a commitment to go to the smaller cities, towns, and villages where there has never been an evangelistic thrust."

In my best Churchillian voice, I promised him blood, sweat, and tears. "It'll be tough. I'm not going to lie to you. It'll be tough, but you'll see people come to Christ."

The challenge appealed to him that night, but before signing him on, I wanted to talk to his wife. So the next time I was in Edmonton I sat down with her and explained the situation. "Red, it's not just Harv that I'm hiring," I told her. "It's both of you. I've got to know that you are happy about Harv working with me. Do you have any problems with this?"

"Well, I really hate to stay alone," she admitted frankly.

"I'll pray about that," I promised her. "You can count on it. Every day that Harv is gone from you I will pray that you will not be lonely."

"Then I'm for it."

And I felt certain God had handpicked just the man to complete our team.

TEN
DAD "JOINS THE TEAM"

"I know you told me I'd have to rough it, but this is ridiculous!" Harvey complained when we were up in Meadow Lake, Saskatchewan. We were staying in a home where the "path" was for real. With no indoor facilities, Harvey had just bundled up for the run to the little house on the back of the lot.

For all the inconveniences we suffered there were compensations. In Meadow Lake the response was so great that the counselors (who had been trained to deal with people coming to make a decision) couldn't keep up with all the inquirers. Harvey was helping out one night, and, standing beside the roaring furnace, he led the local postmaster to the Lord. That made the lack of modern conveniences seem insignificant.

Having to stay in local homes was one of the disadvantages of going to the small, out-of-the-way places where often there would be no hotel; or, sometimes just to cut expenses, the people would put us up. Maybe I should say, *put up* with us, because I'm afraid we were not always the most gracious guests. Our time schedule seldom fit in with that of the hosts. None of the team felt like eating before a meeting, so afterwards, about 9:30 or 10:00 P.M., we were ready for a big meal. Then we would still be wound up and ready to relax a bit. One of our big passions back then was

Crokinole, a board game played by flipping a little disk into a center pocket with your finger, much like my old hockey game. We would play that until one or two in the morning, whooping and hollering, and certainly keeping the household awake. Then we'd sleep until ten the next day while the family had to get up for work or school.

Most of the homes were quite comfortable, and the hosts extremely gracious. But there were exceptions. In one Saskatchewan town, Harvey was quartered downstairs in a coal bin—literally. There was no longer any coal stored down there, but the rafters, splinters, and floor were all the same. I, being the chief, got the little attic room with the pitched roof for a ceiling.

In Hanna, Alberta, in January of 1962, it was so cold there was frost on the insides of the walls. Missionaries delight in returning from the foreign field and telling tales of how tough living conditions were, but we could match them story for story. We were on a mission field without ever leaving the continent.

One of the big things Schroeder had going for him was his sense of humor. He has some routines that match anything Red Skelton or Bob Hope ever came up with. And to ensure the choir members arriving on time, he would go through one of his monologues at the beginning of rehearsal each evening. No one ever came late after the first night, whether it was the 400-voice choir in Winnipeg, or a handful in Podunk Hollow.

If we hadn't been able to laugh and play and pray together, Harvey, Lyall, and I would never have made it on those long tours that threw us together for up to five weeks at a time. To save a buck on transportation, Blackwood would schedule us for a series of meetings in the same end of the country. It would save money, but it was difficult for us to be away from our families for so long. And it was hard on our women at home holding down the fort.

In some of the larger crusades Blackwood would be with us for at least part of the time, and we picked up local musical talent wherever we went. Whether it was just Lyall, Harv, and myself, or a whole gang, the team would get together every day for prayer. First we would review what had happened, give special emphasis to any prayer requests we had received, analyze the situation (Was the weather a factor? Were we competing with a local sports event that night?) and remind ourselves why we were there.

"Just because this is a small town, the folks are just as lost here as they are in the big city," I'd remind them. "We had 12,000 in Winnipeg, and only 600 here last night, but figure the averages. Six hundred is a third of this 'Mud-ville' and 12,000 in Winnipeg is peanuts. We're having a real impact on this community."

Friday nights were always "youth nights" and Lyall and the musicians would stay and help Harv and me as we attempted to entertain the teens for a purpose. Coming right after a crusade meeting, we were always exhausted when these started, but the kids would be full of energy and delighted with having us spend the time with them.

Then the next morning we would have our "Uncle Barry and Uncle Harv" show for the children. A regular routine developed between us. We didn't have a written script, and we didn't rehearse it—it just sort of evolved. The focal point was a fish bowl of candy. I'd have a handful of pennies, back when kids could buy something with a penny, and I'd consider adding the pennies to the candy. "Hey, you're kidding," Uncle Harv would say. "Are you really going to put all those pennies in, too?" And the kids would all yell, "Yeah! Yeah! Put the pennies in." So I'd sprinkle the pennies in with the salt-water taffy.

Out would come my little red New Testament. "I have here a magic book," I would convince them. "It's going to give the row and seat number of the youngster who is going to come down here and grab as much candy as his fist will hold. But remember, it is a magic book, and it never calls for anyone who is not paying attention!" Boy, would they pay attention.

"Rrrrrow forty-one!" I'd call out. "Uncle Harv, count the rows and find number forty-one."

Harv would start counting the rows out loud, and they'd all join in, but he would go forty ... forty-one ... forty-two ... forty-three, and keep on counting until he had counted himself out the door. The kids would all be twisting around, wondering where he had gone. Then he would reappear, all out of breath. "Uncle Hucklebarry, there isn't any row 141."

"I said row forty-one, not 141."

"Oh," and he would start all over again.

"And it is seat number . . . fifteen!" and on and on. Then we'd sing a bunch of action choruses such as "Deep and Wide." I'd tell them a story, short and to the point. I'd try to make it crystal clear, but I never made it easy for them. I'd ask them to pray quietly. After the prayer, I'd say, "Now Uncle Harv and Uncle Lyall are going to be at the door with the bowls of candy. As you leave, everyone will get some." Then, as if it were an afterthought, I'd add, "Oh, it may well be that some of you boys and girls prayed that prayer. We'd like to talk to you about it. All those who prayed and really meant it, you come sit up here."

This would be a deterrent for them, since the candy was at the door for those who were leaving. But they would come to the front and stay in droves. I get rather turned off by statistics. Numbers alone seem cold and lifeless; yet there were hundreds of children who came to know the Lord during those Saturday morning meetings. There *was* warmth and genuineness in those decisions; and the children got their candy afterwards.

The response at those meetings primed us for the closing services of the crusade when it seemed the meetings were always packed to the rafters. We would be exalting over the final windup when it came time to split up and go home to our own children.

"Tell Little Red I've been praying for her," I'd frequently remind Harv. Then I'd head for the "forest city"—London, Ontario.

I hadn't been an evangelist long before I realized I was living two separate lives. Audrey soon learned that it took me awhile to acclimate myself to the home situation after I'd been gone. When I first hit the door, all I wanted was a hug and a welcome home. Then the next day she could tell me about the dripping faucet or the window with a crack in it.

We also learned quickly that it didn't work to save discipline problems for my return. We tried that for a while, but it made the kids dread my return, and I didn't feel like lighting into them after not seeing them for weeks.

Our kids reacted very differently to my being gone so much. Kerry Jane was old enough to understand, and being the sweetheart she is, I think she rather enjoyed her role as mother's helper. Mark and I had become pretty good buddies during the two years we lived in South Carolina, and now I felt he resented my absence. Little Timmy had never known any other life, and seemed to take it for granted that fathers disappear for weeks at a time.

For Butch, the added responsibilities she took on because of my ministry were part of her dedication to the Lord. She didn't complain, and never, never said, "Don't go. I want you to be with me that week," or "Get it over with and come home and help me." Because I was gone so much, she didn't feel it was fair to the kids to become too involved in outside activities. So she restricted herself to teaching Sunday school, because the children were involved in that also.

There were many social situations in which she wouldn't want to go out alone, and times when she would have liked to entertain, but without me, didn't. Then when I'd get home, I'd want to park a bit. I sure didn't feel like going out, so she'd stay with me.

Then there was the feeling that I couldn't share my other life with my family. I would have loved to take them along on some of the trips so they could see what a glorious country we live in. There were friends scattered across the Dominion that I couldn't introduce to my family. This might sound as if I'm feeling sorry for myself, but I'm just trying to give a realistic picture. The life of an evangelist is not all glamour and pats on the back. There's a price to pay for the privilege of being in his service.

Then I'd go over to the office and Blackwood would say, "Look at the invitations that have come in this week," or "Read this letter about a family that was turned around after the crusade last month," or, "The list of regular supporters is growing steadily." Every time I would hit the pits, the Lord would send me some encouragement.

The office ran smooth as silk. I marveled at Jim's efficiency and his phenomenal capacity for remembering details. If I ever doubted I was in the right business, I would consider the caliber of men the Lord had put on my team and be reassured. The work had grown so that we needed a full-time man to act as crusade director. I'd invited Herb Bock to join the team after the masterful job he did as chairman of the second Regina crusade. But being a spiritual man, he had merely replied, "I'll pray about it."

While I was home I'd try to make up for lost time by being with the kids as much as possible. We'd throw a football around, or play games. Kerry Jane was well coordinated and could have been an excellent athlete if she hadn't been such a feminine young lady. Mark was exceptional in every sport he tried, but didn't like to take any tips from his old man. Tim, as the youngest, seemed a bit awed by the capabilities of his older siblings. But he was a tough little guy and he'd try.

One thing I always did before I left town was to place a phone number where I could be reached next to the telephone. I tried to reassure the kids that even though I wasn't there, I was just a call away, and in case of a real emergency I would be home as fast as an airplane would fly me.

The first time that emergency number was ever used I was in Shag Harbor, Nova Scotia.

It was Blackwood who made the call. "Your father's had a stroke," he said kindly. "Better try to get home if you want to see him again."

Getting out of Shag Harbor wasn't the easiest thing to do. First I had to get someone to drive me to Halifax, then get a plane to Montreal, fly to Toronto, and on to London. The trip took a whole day and I was concerned that I wouldn't get home in time to tell my father good-bye. He had always been so strong and healthy that it was hard for me to realize that he was at the point of death.

Butch was waiting for me when I stepped off the plane and we drove directly to Langarth Street where my father was lying in his bed in the middle bedroom. He was pale and lifeless looking, and his breathing was very shallow. He couldn't move or speak, and I didn't know if he realized I was there or not. I took one of his hands in mine and sat there a while.

His hand seemed rather symbolic to me. He'd been the first one to teach me to catch a ball, but when I got so I could zing 'em back to him, he had to quit playing catch with me, because he couldn't take the risk of getting his hands injured. A linotype operator with a broken finger would be out of a job.

Scenes of him walking hand in hand with Kerry Jane when she was a toddler came back to me. I remembered how he and Mark would make a game of throwing popsicle sticks into a gully behind the ice cream store in South Carolina. I could visualize him pushing little Timmy on the old swing behind his house.

"He's got two or three days," was the doctor's prediction.

My mother was beside herself. She had always been very dependent on my father, and I couldn't imagine her coping alone. In a situation like that there is nothing you can do but pray. And I prayed.

By the next morning he seemed to have rallied some and the doctor changed his prognosis. "He's in no imminent danger of death and he could stay in this condition for weeks. Months."

Even with that reassurance, it was hard to leave Dad, but I felt I had to get back to the crusade since I had left Schroeder and Conlin in the lurch. "From now on I'll always keep a spare sermon in my hip pocket," Harv told me. "Just in case of another emergency."

"How did the meeting go without me?"

"Fine. Good crowd. They came expecting you. I gave them some extra music and for once they got a sermon of the desired length."

"All right, this is no time to start needling me about the length of my sermons," I declared, acting all indignant. The team members were always dropping hints about long messages, but I didn't get any complaints from the converts. I felt I should take as long as necessary to make the message clear.

133

From Shag Harbor we went directly to Sherbrooke, Quebec, so I didn't return home for ten more days. By that time my father had been moved to the hospital. After a few weeks there, he was moved to a convalescent home a mile or so from Langarth Street. My "dependent" mother was rising to the occasion, and was not only keeping up with the house, but was walking to the home every day to be with Dad. Since she didn't have a car, and no bus service was available, she would make the hike twice a day on her own. I was glad it was spring and the weather was so nice.

Visiting with Dad in that place was depressing. He had always been so alive and vital, as though he were a part of nature. Now his garden was going to seed and the weeds were taking over his meticulously trimmed lawn. "Lo, Shon," he managed to say to me in a very labored greeting. I went by every evening while I was home, but before I left for the next crusade I had a request for him. "Dad, I want you to pray for me. I'll be in a little town in Southern Michigan for five days. When I get home, I'll come give you a report. All right?"

He nodded his agreement with the most enthusiasm he'd displayed since his stroke, and the bargain was sealed. From that time on we had a partnership going. He was the prayer partner for our team, and he looked forward to my reports more than the sports news or the occasional rides he was allowed to take.

"We really had an unusual experience this time," I told him that fall. "Sunday night I preached to 4,200 in the Exhibition Stadium in Saskatoon, Saskatchewan, and Tuesday night I stood before forty-two people in Uranium City."

"U-u-ran-ium?" he questioned.

"Yeah, Uranium City. It's right up by the border of the Northwest Territories. About as far north as you can go without getting cold. We had hundreds of decisions in Saskatoon, and then Harvey, Lyall, and I took an El Dorado Airlines plane to Fort Smith right on the border line of Alberta and the Northwest Territories. From there, to get to Uranium City you either fly in a little puddle jumper, or you take a dog sled. So we got on this plane where you serve your own coffee and you tiptoe around the machinery and canned goods and luggage.

"Well, the population of Uranium City is only about 1400, mostly miners, and we found out that the only radio they have is a single channel CBC satellite. The last night they let us have the radio time, and my sermon was piped into the mines. The next day I got the reaction from some of the miners who had been a captive audience thousands of feet below the earth. 'You cracker!' one said. 'Here we are down in the bowels of the earth and you preach on hell!'"

My dad laughed! He loved that story, and it was reassuring to see that his sense of humor hadn't been paralyzed.

"Well, then we had to get back into that twelve-seater plane with all the freight and take off on a runway that deadends at a lake. Either the plane takes off, or you go right into the drink. You know what a white-knuckle flier I am anyway. Well, I didn't feel very secure in that plane, I kid you not. So we sat behind the cargo, right near the door, but the door wouldn't close! There was no latch, so they tied it shut. Tied the rope around the handle, then across the cabin to the other side, then back across the cabin again to the cargo.

"When we took off they couldn't pressurize the cabin because of the door, so they flew below 4,000 feet the whole way. The rope was vibrating, causing a high-pitched whistle throughout the cabin that was disconcerting, to say the least. Well, the farther we went, the more that rope worked itself loose, and the pitch of the whistle got lower and lower. I was getting more and more nervous about the situation, and that character Schroeder reminds me of the Canadian Pacific airliner that had a door come open and people were sucked out. I really needed that! But, praise God, we made it. You must have been praying for us, Dad."

He grinned his lopsided smile and nodded his head.

We were doing a crusade in Kitchener, practically in my backyard, when Lyall informed me, "This will be my last crusade."

"What?"

"Well, I've been on the road ever since we were married, and now that Colleen is expecting I want to be with her," he explained.

I was deeply disappointed. The Moore, Blackwood, Schroeder, Conlin team had been set in concrete as far as I was concerned. Bringing in guests for special appearances was one thing, but I had never anticipated the team splitting up.

Mervin Saunders from Ottawa served as organist for a couple of meetings. For the eight-day Calgary Crusade in the Jubilee Auditorium we added a young pianist from the Alliance church named Roy Morden. The first time I had heard Roy play was at a YFC camp back when he was a teenager. Schroeder had known him for years and was very impressed with his abilities. The musical program was also enhanced by the glorious voice of a black tenor soloist named Jimmy McDonald.

Another organist we used that year was Leslie Grant from the Stone Church in Toronto. Schroeder promptly nicknamed him Stubby, and he seemed to fit in quite well. He was excellent at the keyboard, but fell asleep during one of my sermons and missed his cue to start playing "Just As I Am." He took our kidding about that quite well, so when we were in St. Catharine's a couple of months later I asked him, "Would you ever be interested in joining a team like this full time?"

"Why don't you ask me?"

We had a new musician.

My father's condition remained stabilized, and my mother's devotion to him unwavering. Whenever I was in town I would make it a practice to stop off and see him for a few minutes on my way home from the office. I'd try to come up with some little story to amuse him. "Say, Dad, did I ever tell you about the time I met one of my converts in a restaurant?"

"Eh?"

"He was one of 'my' converts all right. I doubt if the Holy Spirit would claim that one. See, I came down to the Victoria Café for breakfast about 10:30 one morning and sitting in the booth across the aisle from me were two winos. This one guy was so out of it, his nose was in his soup. After a few minutes he looked over my way and exclaimed, 'Why, it's Barry! The real Barry Moore.' Then he yells over at me, 'Hey, Barry, c'mon over here. I, hic, want you to meet my buddy.'

"Well, needless to say, I was embarrassed and tried to ignore the guy. Then, wouldn't you know, he gets up and staggers over to my booth, and in full voice proclaims, 'Shey, Barry! God bless you, Barry! I've been over to the meetins. C'mon over here, I want you to meet my buddy. Ah'm trying to win him to the Lord.'"

Dad laughed and asked, "Wa ja do?"

"Well, I went over and met him. What else could I do? I tried to give a sober witness, but I don't think he was thinking clearly enough to understand."

The team had learned by this time to request hotel accommodations whenever possible so that we could have a room to ourselves. Even then we sometimes wound up in some flea-bitten place with one bathroom for the whole floor. We were in one where the facilities were so small you had to back in and then shut the door. I had to wonder how Stubby fit. Jimmy McDonald was with us on that trip, and he wised up and checked out the difference in price at a new modern hotel down the street. I then explained to the local chairman that we would pay the difference so that we could take showers after the meeting.

"Oh, but you couldn't afford that!"

"But it's only one dollar difference."

"Is that all? Well, certainly, move. We'll pick up the tab."

It continued to amaze me how God opened so many doors for us. We were getting in places where there had never been a city-wide crusade before. Many were out in pioneer areas with small populations, but we'd draw from the surrounding area and have crowds larger than anyone could have anticipated. I remember coming back and telling Dad about one meeting that had been productive beyond my faith. "Three hundred more in the kingdom, Dad."

"Prery good. Prery good."

The ministry was going so "good" that Blackwood resigned his work with YFC so he could work full time. This was shortly after Herb Bock finally got finished praying and joined our team. From then on Blackwood would do the advance work, schedule our meetings, and handle things in the office. Herb would go into each crusade location a few days ahead of the rest of the team to make sure everything was running smoothly. He'd take care of followup and details concerning ancillary meetings.

We were in Prince Albert, Saskatchewan, in the middle of winter one time and a lady asked me, "Why aren't you in Florida? I thought all evangelists headed south for the winter."

"Well, there are two good reasons that I can think of," I told her. "Number one is, nobody has invited me to Florida; and number two is, in the summertime all the farmers are out on the prairies taking advantage of the long days. If you want to reach them you have to do it in their off season."

"Well, I for one appreciate your coming and braving our weather," she declared.

I appreciated her saying that, and often remembered it when hit by some particularly frigid blast. There was one good feature about having summer as the off-season. That was having more time during the months the kids were out of school. The older they got, the more I appreciated those summers we rented a cottage at Ipperwash with its beautiful sandy beach. It isn't really possible to make up for lost time with your youngsters, but I tried.

It was always good to have some relaxed time with Blackwood to talk and dream and make plans for the future. "We now have fifty-four invitations for future crusades," he mentioned to me once quite casually.

"Fifty-four! How many of those are small places?"

"Well, our average is running consistent. Half of the eighteen crusades last year were in communities of 5,000 or less. I was compiling some statistics for the annual report the other day and we've had nearly 7,000 inquirers for salvation. That's not counting all the other decisions made during the crusades."

"That's why it doesn't get old," I exclaimed. "After eighty some crusades now, each time we begin another series of meetings I feel just as excited and challenged as I was the first year. I get tired of the road, and I'm always anxious to get home to my family, but the responses we've seen just keep the ol' adrenaline pumping."

"Can't you two ever do anything but talk shop?" Butch would wail. We'd look at each other, grin, and just shrug our shoulders. We felt we were involved in the most exciting business in the world, and it was hard to imagine a more interesting topic. The whole team felt the same way. At least I thought so, until Harvey made his big announcement.

"This is going to be my last crusade," he said calmly, and the earth stood still. At least I thought it did.

"You're kidding?"

"Well, I have a tremendous offer from Calvary Temple in Denver, Colorado. I'll be the Minister of Music, in charge of eleven choirs. . . ."

"And the pay's better," I added cryptically.

"Couldn't be much worse," he laughed. "I've been on the road five years now. Little Red is expecting, and I need to be with her."

"Has she ever been lonely?"

"No, she says she never has. But I need to be with Karen and Darrell more, too, That isn't the only reason for going, Barry. I've sincerely prayed about this and I feel that's where the Lord is leading me. I wouldn't go otherwise, you know that."

I still couldn't believe it. We were the consummate duo. How could he break us up? I couldn't accept his decision as final, and I tried my best to dissuade him. But he was determined.

"But think of the way God has blessed our efforts," I reminded him. "And we've had some pretty good times along the way, too."

"Yeah. Yeah, Barry, that's true," he agreed, nodding his head. "Nobody has ever had more fun winning souls to Jesus than we have."

And that was it. My soul brother was off the team. "Hey, if you ever need help, I'll be available to you," he promised. And he was gone.

At least I was certain I could depend on Blackwood's loyalty.

ELEVEN
STORMY WEATHER

When the invitation came to attend the World Congress on Evangelism in Berlin, Germany, I was pleased. There was going to be a gathering of several thousand evangelists from one hundred different countries, and it was an honor to be one of those chosen to represent Canada. Quite frankly, I felt I deserved the opportunity for a European jaunt with my contemporaries. I'd been conducting crusades full time for six years, and had picked up a bit of information about mass evangelism. But I was always eager to learn more. Besides, I hadn't been to Europe for a whole decade.

The personnel problems that had plagued us at the beginning of the year had been settled. I discovered after Schroeder left that it was all right to bring in soloists or musicians on a "guest" basis, doing one or two crusades now and then. But it just didn't work with my music master. I had to have a full-time platform man who could work with the choir, emcee the program, and lead congregational singing. To run a coordinated program we had to be able to anticipate each other. The answer to those prayers had been Donald Jost, who joined the team in January of 1966. The skill he had acquired directing choral groups since high school, his educational background at Briercrest Bible Institute, and his experience pastoring churches and carrying a daily radio program all combined to make Jost eminently qualified. Besides, we got along pretty well together.

We'd been using Ed Lyman as our "guest" soloist for most of the larger meetings, and he added a touch of class to the team. With an operatic background and the years of training that entails, he had to be considered one of the most outstanding tenor soloists in the field of gospel music. He'd sung on the U.S. Armed Forces TV Network in Bermuda and the Canal Zone and had become known as "The Singing Marine."

All that and a good sense of humor, too. He could swap tall stories with the best of them, and had spent time in Youth For Christ, so we had many friends in common. With Lyman as soloist, Jost leading the music, Bock directing the crusades, and Blackwood holding down the fort, I felt secure about the all-pro team backing me up.

So, going to Berlin seemed feasible, if the money was available. I didn't want to dip into the cash flow of the organization, so I decided I would write a letter to a few select friends and share the opportunity with them. If they felt moved to come up with the necessary funds, I'd go. If not, I'd conclude it wasn't meant to be.

The return mail brought enough to cover all my expenses, and I made reservations. My itinerary was set up with a stopover in London, England, where I spoke at a youth meeting. Then I flew to Barcelona, Spain, to visit with some missionary friends. I went on to Rome, where I spoke at the Italian Bible Institute of the Greater Europe Mission. Then to Geneva, Switzerland. By the time I landed in Berlin I was feeling quite the globe-trotting big-wheel evangelist.

It was after 10 P.M. when I checked into the Congress Hall, where I was informed that I would have to take a cab to the Hilton. I went out front, carrying my bags, and spotted a couple of guys getting into a taxi. Since I overheard one of them tell the cabbie they wanted to go to the Hilton, I called out, "Oh, are you going to the Hilton?"

"Yes, are you?"

"Yes, I am. May I . . . ?"

"By all means; get in the back."

I climbed into the back and sat next to an elderly gentleman with his collar up around his neck. The man in front turned around and said, "I'm David Hubbard, president of Fuller Seminary. Have you met Dr. Fuller?"

I shook hands with Charles E. Fuller, and all of a sudden I was small potatoes. It seems every time I get to thinking I'm someone, the Lord lets something happen to get me back into perspective.

The Berlin Congress had a great effect on my life. There was a breaking down of denominationalism. Factions that had been created by misunderstanding and misconception of others' motives were dissolved. There was a union of spirit and purpose without compromise or ecclesiastical organization.

One event that especially touched me was the appearance of two Auca Indians from the jungles of Ecuador standing on the platform. They were with the sister of one of the five missionaries who had been slain ten years before, while trying to take the gospel to that remote tribe. The older of the two men, Kimo, was one of the murderers. He gave his testimony and Rachel Saint translated his words. It was amazing to listen to the evident transformation in this man's heart as he told of his desire to tell his former enemies of the Son of the Great God.

When the testimonies were over, the Aucas returned to their places. But before the chairman could pronounce the benediction, a Nigerian evangelist rose to his feet and raced to the platform. As he publicly embraced the Aucas, a great chorus of "Amens" rang across the assembly hall. I'll never forget the breaking down of racial barriers that took place as that black man expressed his love and appreciation for the two bronze-skinned Indians and the white woman who had shared with them the love of God.

I left Berlin with a greater world awareness than I'd ever had. Schroeder had often told me, "The time will come when you are going to have to lift that 'Canadian' label. You'll have far greater opportunities, for your ministry can reach around the world. There's nothing holy about small places." I'd just shrug and tell him, "Now, Harv, we've got to remember the pit from which we were digged." Now I had to consider that maybe he was right. I should at least be willing to go to other countries.

Flying over the Atlantic on my forty-first birthday, I was thankful for the reinforcement I had gotten from the Congress that we were doing some things right. There had been much discussion about the three main criticisms of evangelism. But as I reviewed them, I sincerely felt that we had successfully avoided them all.

The use of excessive emotionalism was an accusation that was discussed, but I had never been accused of that. I always preached for a decision, and I tried my best to make that decision a clear one. Perhaps I made it too much a matter of the intellect, but I wanted people to know what they were doing when they walked forward in one of my meetings. I'd been accused of being tough, because I emphasized repentance. But there was none of that "Do-you-want-to-live-closer-to-God?" business in my sermons.

Another criticism mentioned was about finances. Our team members were all on salary, and none of us were in the five-figure range. Local committees worked out their budgets before we got there. We'd take up collections only if complete campaign funds hadn't been raised in advance. Any extra funds that might come in were turned over to the local committee. There was never a "love offering" for the evangelist or anyone else. An opportunity to donate to the association was given once in every six days of meetings, and it was explained that this was to make it possible for us to go to small towns that could not afford an evangelistic crusade otherwise.

The third criticism was that evangelism was too superficial. But we had done some followup that showed that ninety-six of 112 persons who had made decisions in one crusade had gone on to become members of local churches. My hard line approach during the invitation might not pull as many people forward, but it seemed that those who made commitments meant it. I still heard from thirty of the thirty-three converts in that first crusade in Cabri!

The only conclusion I could draw was that we were doing

something right. The fact that we were booked for a year in advance substantiated that.

I managed to squeeze in forty-eight hours at home before heading to Smiths Falls, Ontario, for my next crusade. From there I spent a couple of days at the Prairie Bible Institute in Three Hills, Alberta, then went to Stettler, Alberta, for the "Heartland Crusade for Christ." When I got home and had time for a breather, I said to Mark, "Hey, man. How about us taking in a Maple Leaf game tonight?"

"Naw, I don't want to go."

I couldn't believe a thirteen-year-old Canadian lad didn't want to see a professional hockey game, so I kept persisting.

"No! I don't want to go with you."

That smarted, but I realized he was just trying to pay me back for all the time I spent away from him. How can you explain to a son who is so like you he seems a mirror image, that you love him, but your commitment to the Lord has to come first? I thought of the hundreds of high school assemblies where I'd spoken and the warm reception I'd gotten from those teens. My recording, "Teacher Talks to Teens" was one of our best sellers, yet I was being rejected by my own son.

It wasn't just the defiance that hurt. Often we would be sitting at the dinner table and the conversation would turn to friends I didn't know, and events I had missed out on. They would laugh at some "in" joke, and I'd sit there with egg on my face. It's rather weird to feel like an outsider with your own family.

When the meal was finished we'd have devotions. Sometimes there would be friends standing outside the back door, waiting for the boys to come play, but my sons knew they would not be excused. First we'd sing something like "Be Like Jesus," or "Heaven Came Down," or "Coming Again." I'd read from M. R. DeHaan's *Daily Bread*, and then we'd pray.

Sometimes it seemed as if I had two families. There was my real family, Audrey and the kids; and the team was the other. That fall Ed Lyman started giving me trouble. Not literally, but he had other paths to pursue and couldn't take as many crusades as I'd have liked him to. Stubby wasn't playing for us much anymore, so we were using Roy Morden and Merv Saunders. I asked them to be on the lookout for some vocal talent. "What we need is someone dumb enough to live on two bucks a day and all he can eat."

Not long after, I got a call from Merv. "I just heard a guy with a great voice. He's just gotten out of the U.S. Air Force. He was one of the Singing Sergeants. He's going to be at the Royal View Church. Why don't you give him a listen?"

Another friend had already mentioned Ken Carter, so I made arrangements to meet him. I went over to the church and this big, strapping, good-looking young guy got up and sang without accompaniment, and the sound rolled around the auditorium. There was no doubt he could sing, so I took him to lunch. He seemed a bit stiff, but with an extrovert like me grilling him, I could understand that. He was young, eager, and dedicated. I figured a few months with the team would take the starch out of him.

Then in January of 1967 Don Kroening accepted the position of accompanist. He was outstanding at either the piano or organ keyboard, and worked well with Carter. At last I felt my team was set and I wouldn't have to be bothered adjusting to new personalities. Bock, Jost, and Kroening were all "Reverends" and I just hoped they wouldn't be so straight-laced that Carter and I couldn't have any fun.

Speaking of fun, Butch and I realized that the summer of 1967 would be the last opportunity we would have to all be together for a family trip. Kerry Jane would graduate from high school in the spring of 1968 and was planning to go right into nurses' training, so we figured we'd make our last summer the best. For years I'd wanted to show them the glories of western Canada, so we planned a trip by auto all the way to Vancouver.

There is nothing that fosters "togetherness" like a 5,000-mile trip by car. Since we stopped and visited friends in a number of places, the trip was not as laborious as it sounds. Kerry Jane and Mark would each take a window in the back of our green Chevy and nine-year-old Tim would get in the middle. When they got tired and wanted to sleep, Mark would lie on the floor, Kerry Jane on the seat, and Timmy would curl up on the back window ledge.

That was really a trip of a lifetime and provided experiences to share with grandchildren someday. Also, I think my kids were impressed that many of the towns we went through had been the scenes of my past crusades, and at how many friends I had across the country.

Inevitably there were a few embarrassing moments. Like when they were asked to stand and be introduced to the congregation of the Alliance Church in Calgary, and Tim let loose a pocketful of little beads he had in his shirt. In the sloping auditorium, they rolled all the way to the front platform.

Then there were the Polish jokes that Mark and Tim continued to quote. They had quite a repertoire, and everywhere we'd stay they would regale the hosts with their recitations. I especially recall them telling stories to Andy and Audrey Govinchuck, who showed us a delightful time in Regina. Andy is a photographer par excellence, and since he has taken a lot of publicity shots of me over the years, I like to keep in his good graces. I need a friendly eye behind the lenses to make me as good looking as possible. When we were getting ready to leave, I wrote their address in my little book and asked, "How do you spell your name? What nationality is that, anyway?"

"Polish."

I was really thankful they were such good sports.

I appreciated the time with my family, but "togetherness" just doesn't work during crusades, and we'd always had an unwritten policy that it would be best not to have our wives with us. I have nothing against women, but I felt when we were going into a town for a crusade we should keep our minds on the task at hand. Then when we were going to Dawson Creek, British Columbia, I got a call from Ken Carter. It seemed that he and his wife, Sherry, were visiting friends in Calgary, Alberta, and he thought that since she was already in that end of the world it might be all right to bring her along. I don't know if I was soft hearted, or soft in the head, but I said "OK."

Well, the minute this gorgeous blonde, who is not much older than my daughter, got off the plane with all her suitcases, I felt I might have made a mistake. Then I realized she was carrying this snuggly little bundle, and I thought, "Good grief, she's brought a baby!" As I got nearer, the bundle began to growl at me and I realized it was a dog! That really burned my bacon, until they explained their friends had just given her the pup, and they were stuck with it.

That really settled it with me as far as bringing wives along was concerned. I didn't bring mine, and it seemed to me that if anyone deserved to travel with us it was Audrey.

The only woman giving me trouble was my mother. For five long years she had gone to the convalescent home every day to be with Dad, and it was affecting her health. Her doctor finally convinced her to cut back her visits to three days a week, but even that was a strain on her. I continued my brief daily visits whenever I was in town. Dad was slowly deteriorating and it was harder and harder to understand what he was trying to say. This was particularly sad because his mind remained alert.

"I've really got some news for you tonight," I told him early in 1969. "The final meeting of the Toronto crusade will be held in the Maple Leaf Gardens." He didn't need any words to express his reaction. It was quite evident by the look on his face that he was thrilled.

So were we. When Blackwood and I had first started contemplating forming an evangelistic association ten years before, we were talking about small, out-of-the-way places, and we had kept to that commitment. Now we had an open door to metro Toronto with 290 churches cooperating. We had never dreamed we would have such an opportunity. The Lord is gracious indeed!

We got good press coverage for the campaign, and had posters, signs, and bumper stickers all over town. Some of the local reporters were obviously skeptical about us filling the arena, but that night 15,000 people filed into the Gardens, while I paced back and forth in a small room under the platform.

I'd preached in pioneer fields from Grand Manan Island

in the Bay of Fundy to Whitehorse in the Yukon Territory. There had been crowds of thousands in hockey arenas, stadiums, and auditoriums from Vancouver to Ottawa. I'd gotten used to setting records, having the largest crowds ever, and making history in cities all across the Dominion, but this was different.

Our team was tops. Each of the men was outstanding in his area of expertise, and we had worked together long enough that we were indeed a team. But this was Maple Leaf Gardens! I'd sat up in those seats and watched the hockey stars who were my heroes as a kid, as they performed on the ice here. I'd seen the arena on television hundreds of times. Here I was, and I was scared.

My knees were trembling when I walked out on the platform. The music and the preliminaries were great; everything went smoothly. I knew there were thousands of people praying for me as I stood alone in the spotlight, and I was still scared. Then as I got into the message, I just relaxed in God, and he took over. It was as if I had jumped into a situation and was in over my head, but he kept me afloat. When the act of witness was given, people streamed down the aisles and I kept saying to myself, "Thank you, God. Thank you."

After that night I was confident nothing could stop my ministry. Well, some big scandal or something might, but I certainly wasn't going to let that happen. We had bookings for over a year ahead. I had a solid, talented, loyal team working with me, and we were going to win the world. Then, late in 1969, we were booked into Augusta, Maine.

We had all gone to Howard Johnson's for a bite to eat after the crusade and then returned to our hotel rooms. I put my key in the door and pushed it open while bending to pick up my briefcase—when I realized there was someone lying in my bed. And it looked an awful lot like "Goldilocks."

"Shoot! I've got the wrong room," I whispered.

"Check your key," Jost suggested.

I looked at my key, 225, then at the door, 225. "It's my room all right. What in the world is going on?"

The fellows began gathering around to find out what my

149

problem was. All I could figure was some unscrupulous person was trying to set me up so that he could tarnish my ministry. "You guys all stay with me," I ordered. "There's a woman in my bed!"

They were all about to choke on their tonsils, but I didn't see any humor in the situation. The bathroom light had been left on, giving just enough light to illuminate the curvaceous figure and blonde hair of the female curled up in the bed. There were towels spread around, and it looked like a setup if ever I'd seen one.

"I don't know what you guys are laughing at! Bock, this is not funny! Who let that woman in my room?"

"Hello!" I called. "Hello," a little louder, but there was no movement. Kroening came out of his room then and wanted to know what was going on. "I don't know, Don. This is my room. I left my clothes in there, and now they are gone and there is a woman in the bed!"

"You had better go in there and get her out of your room," Jost suggested.

"Oooooeee! I'm not going in there," I exploded. "You go get her out."

About this time Carter reached in and turned on the light. It was a mannequin! "You dirty guys!" Boy, I let them have it with every ecclesiastical expletive I could come up with. "You cotton pickers!" Did they laugh! They thought they'd pulled the greatest practical joke of all time. I looked out the glass doors, and there across the courtyard I could see the night clerk in the office, falling off his chair laughing. I shook my fist at him, and he laughed all the harder.

When I finally cooled down a bit, one of the guys reached under the bed and pulled out a tape recorder. They had all my reactions on tape! They played it over and just howled! And I had once wondered if this bunch might be too straight-laced!

It's mind boggling to consider that God could use a bunch of characters like that for his glory. Yet we had a great crusade there. The National Guard Armory was at capacity the last three nights and we had over 300 decisions that week. The Lord can use anyone. At least the incident was an indication of the kind of rapport we had on the team. Then everything started falling apart.

First Carter came and announced Sherry was expecting and wanted him to be with her when she had the baby. "We just can't live on what I'm making," he told me. "Not and feed a baby, too."

Then it was Don Jost. He decided he wanted to go back into the pastorate. He had mentioned this from time to time, and I wasn't as surprised about it. But when Kroening decided to leave too, I began to think there was a conspiracy afoot.

What was even more unimaginable was that Blackwood and I weren't getting along. Call it a personality clash or whatever. All I know is we had been buddies for years and now it seemed to me he wanted to run everything his way. I realized that in leaving the details to him, little by little I had lost control of the organization of which I was supposed to be president. I had committed my ministry to him, but now it seemed as if the whole organization was pivoting around him.

The big clash came when we got in an argument over a Christian magazine he wanted to start. I said, "No, that isn't our thing." We both got pretty heated up and raised our voices. That sent me reeling mentally. First all the guys leaving and now this!

It may sound paranoid, but I started wondering if perhaps there was a conspiracy against me. Was my ministry over? Had God turned his back on me? I went into a period of spiritual agony that lasted for months. I began to lose weight, I couldn't sleep, and I'd drink Maalox as if it were soda pop. During this time I began having Audrey type my business letters at home, because I felt more and more uncomfortable at the office.

I'd leave for a crusade feeling heartsick. One of the most amazing things about this whole episode was that even though I was at my lowest ebb spiritually, I'd stand behind those pulpits feeling weak in mind, body and spirit, and the Holy Spirit would take over. If ever I needed proof that conversions are a result of the wooing of the Spirit and the power of the Word, this showed me. People were coming to Christ in spite of the preacher. It certainly was in no way because of any strength of my own.

In June Kerry Jane graduated from nursing school. I flew home at my own expense from Rockland, Maine, so I could be there for the event. We had a reception in her honor in our home following the graduation exercises. It was a relaxing time of fun and fellowship, and naturally we had invited the Blackwoods; they had known Kerry Jane since she was a child. Jim chose that night to inform me of his decision to resign.

I didn't know what to do. I spent a sleepless night worrying about it. The resignation was to take effect August 31. Maybe Jim was right. Maybe I couldn't make it without him. I knew I wasn't much of a businessman, and I certainly didn't know the office routine. Maybe I should call him and eat crow, or ask his forgiveness and promise to let him have complete control in the future. I cried, and prayed and paced the floor, but no answer came.

The next morning I was talking it over with Audrey and I finally decided I'd just have to swallow my pride and beg Jim to stay.

"Oh, no, you won't!" The steel in my meek little wife's voice brought me up sharp. "You are not wrong, and you are not going to apologize!" The situation had tested Audrey's mettle, too. She was stronger than I'd dreamed.

Feeling as emotionally drained as I ever had in my life, I got on a plane and flew back to the crusade in Maine. That night I preached on "The Dropout Takes a Trip," the story of the Prodigal Son. It was a sermon I'd preached many times before, and as my mind slipped into gear, the words tumbled out. There were many decisions that night, and it certainly was not the power of a persuasive personality that wooed them.

Herb Bock was directing the crusade, and I shared with him the agony I'd been suffering over Jim's resignation. At least now our differences were out in the open and I felt free to discuss it without being disloyal. It seemed everyone I told about the problem would bring up the dissension between Paul and Barnabas. I really got tired of people mentioning that, because every time I heard it I thought, "Yeah, and one of them was never heard of again."

I had the whole summer to chew on that resignation. Over and over I thought, "If my God isn't big enough to overrule in this situation, then he isn't big enough." God had to be the answer, but I couldn't seem to get in touch with him. I prayed and prayed, often lying prostrate on the floor, pouring my heart out. I'd tried with everything within me to serve him, and now it seemed he'd turned his back on me. Everyone was leaving me. Even the office staff was going to go with Jim to set up a new work.

Audrey was a brick. No man ever had a wife more faithful and loyal. Without her unquestioning support throughout that trial I just might have lost my mind. She listened patiently as I went over the problem again and again. For a gal who had married a school teacher, expecting to live a normal, secure life, she certainly got a lot more than she had bargained for.

On August 11, shortly before Blackwood's resignation was to take effect, I noticed a little item in the "25 YEARS AGO" column in *The London Free Press.* "London Majors won two Intercounty ball games, defeating Galt 8-2 at Galt in the afternoon with Barry Moore pitching." Twenty-five years. A lifetime ago. My love for the game had never abated, and I had to wonder how different my life would have been if I had chosen to follow my natural inclination toward sports instead of full-time evangelistic work. My life wouldn't be in the mess it was at the moment, yet I still felt I had chosen the right path. I felt akin to Job, who had said, "Though God slay me, yet will I trust him."

I had the strongest desire to talk with Harvey Schroeder. Harv had always accepted me just as I was. He never expected me to be perfect, or holier than the next guy. He'd kept in touch with me ever since he'd left the team, and I knew I could trust him. He had all his marbles in a row, and I felt that if anyone could help me through this, it would be Harv.

On my next trip to the States I made arrangements for a side trip to Denver. Harv met me at the airport and I began pouring my heart out to him. When I finally wound down, I let out a long sigh, then waited for some consolation.

"Barry," he said, "don't sweat the small stuff."

Mark Moore at the Windsor Crusade, Sept. 1981.

TWELVE
GOD KEEPS
HIS PROMISES

"Barry, the gift is yours, and the ministry is yours, and the demand for the gift would exist with no assistants at all," Schroeder insisted. "I've told you for years that if you ever needed me, I'd be there to help. OK, give me a few months to wind things up here, and I'll be your man."

"You really will?" I could hardly believe my ears. Schroeder was doing a great work at Calvary Temple. He had eleven choirs with over 500 people enrolled in the music program. He had even directed the Denver Symphony Orchestra.

"And I'll tell you something else," he continued. "I have an idea your ministry is not only going to continue, but it is going to thrive. We're rather goal oriented at Calvary, so just for the sake of measurement, let's say your ministry is going to increase by 20 percent a year."

I couldn't believe that either, but it sure was good to hear. I needed that encouragement. I needed someone who believed in me. When the Lord promised to supply all our needs, I don't think he meant only money.

Another position that needed to be filled was business manager or executive director. Whatever it was called, I needed someone in the office. Herb Bock came to mind. Certainly he knew the work; he had been directing all my crusades since he signed on in 1964. Bock had a pastor's heart, was excellent at handling people, and was on a first-name basis with every evangelical pastor in Canada— or so it seemed. But as a businessman? For that matter, he might not even want to stay with a sinking ship. I put in a call.

"Barry, I'm staying," Herb said, and a firmness was evident in his soft voice. "And I want you to know it is not just a matter of friendship, but because of a conviction that the ministry must continue."

"Would you be willing to move to London and take over the operation from here?"

There was a pause. I knew Herb and his wife. Both their families were from the west, and moving to Ontario with their five children would be a difficult proposition.

"I'll talk to Delly, and we'll pray about it and let you know."

The response was no surprise. What did amaze me was that Bock proved to be much more of a businessman than I had ever imagined. He got into that office, reorganized filing systems, delegated authority to new secretarial help he hired, and was full of ideas to improve the management aspects of the organization. It was evident, however, that he couldn't keep up with all the office work and carry on the load as crusade director at the same time. We needed another man.

Not two days after Bock was settled in London, I got a call from Toronto from Bernie Camper. Now Bernie was a representative of Bata Shoes in the West Indies whom I had met during a crusade in Jamaica. So I was rather surprised to hear he was in Toronto.

"We're planning to move to Canada," he informed me.

"Have you a job in mind?"

"Not yet, but I'm sure something will show up."

"How'd you like to come and help me?"

Things were beginning to fall into place too beautifully to be mere coincidence. Bernie had had years of experience in business and advertising—just what we needed. We set it up so Bock was vice-president and Camper was executive director.

Then we made contact with a singer named Art Perri.

That was strictly a provision of the Lord. Art is a wild, fun-loving, emotional Italian with such a joy for living that he nearly makes the air sparkle. Funny! He and Schroeder would start clowning around after the service and make me laugh.

Even the laughter seemed a provision from the Lord, because I had been deeply hurt, and the laughter helped to heal the wounds. The people who can hurt you the most are those you love the most, and Blackwood and I had been buddies for a long time. Comrades-in-arms. Partners. His leaving, I felt, was a desertion, and I'll always carry the scars from that. But the Lord was faithful, and in spite of all the turmoil, he continued to use me and teach me.

It was about this time that the Lord gave me the thirty-seventh Psalm as my own. "Rest in the Lord." "Cease from anger." "Forsake wrath." The phrases leaped out at me as I read and reread the Psalm and began praying for peace. I realized that to continue worrying over what had happened was useless. It didn't really matter who was right and who was wrong. Our pathways had separated, but the Lord was continuing to use us both. On my daily prayer list I wrote, "Lord, give me peace and complete confidence in you."

Another of the "encouragers" the Lord gave me during my time of spiritual turmoil was Doug Hindmarsh, the director of the Eastern Division of Reimer Express. Doug had served as publicity chairman for the Toronto crusade and we had become close friends following that initial contact. His willingness to use his business acumen for the Lord's work had brought him invitations to serve on the board of a number of Christian organizations. When I explained the organizational problems we were having, he promised to come on our board, despite his heavy commitments elsewhere. True to his word, he gave the board some very able direction in enabling us to "broaden our base."

Lloyd Rapson was another rock the Lord sent me when I felt my own foundations were shaky. Lloyd was a local businessman who made himself available to me. When I needed a sounding board, a willing listener who would neither judge nor criticize, Lloyd was there. He also pitched in and helped the board restructure itself.

We broadened the base of the board by replacing those who left with new men from across the Dominion rather than limiting ourselves to the Ontario area. We broadened our prayer support, our financial base, and the contact and followup procedures. A benefit program was set up for all our employees to include health, welfare, and pension programs.

Those were busy days, but productive and rewarding. Before I realized it the first year was gone and Herb Bock was standing in the doorway of my office, beaming.

"What's up?"

"Barry, I've just been compiling the annual statistics. Would you believe, we are up 20 percent in every category?"

"What? No kidding?"

"Yep! Up 20 percent in decisions, income, supporters, the works."

"Wait until Schroeder hears this. Will he cackle!"

That was one "I told you so" that I enjoyed as much as Harvey did. Schroeder is really a great encourager, and a good guy to have around. I think he also likes to be a peacemaker, and from time to time he would drop subtle little ideas like, "I found it interesting that Jost lasted five years before he'd had enough, the same length of time I took it. Five years of running from pillar to post wears thin on you. All that travel and being away from your family and all. Yet Blackwood lasted ten."

Another time it was, "You know, the guys in the office do an awful lot of work, yet they don't get the laurels. You get the pats on the back, and for a special guy like Bock that's fine. But most people need encouraging once in a while. The guy that is behind the scenes doesn't get noticed if everything is running smoothly."

It was obvious what he was getting at, but I wasn't ready. Besides, I was working on my relationship with my children. Kerry Jane was doing fine working as a nurse at St. Joseph's hospital, and I felt we were friends. The boys were old enough now that I could take them with me occasionally. The summer of 1970 Tim had spent time with me at a youth camp in the Muskokas while I served as conference speaker. The next summer I took Mark and Paul Whitelaw, Kerry Jane's latest boyfriend, with me to Jamaica for my first crusade at Christiana. Mark played his guitar and swam all day and seemed to enjoy himself.

Mark seemed to be making progress in his Christian walk. He had made a profession of faith as a child, but at seventeen he committed his life to Christ's control at a YFC camp. Since then he'd been playing his guitar and singing with a Christian group called "The Carpenter's Union." I wasn't really into their kind of music, and I thought Mark wore his hair too long, but those were superficial disagreements. I was proud of his musical ability and the fact that he was using his talent for the Lord.

The invitations for crusades were coming at such a pace that we needed to enlarge our staff, and I always kept an eye open for a good man. When I met the Canadian director of the Gospel Missionary Union, Mark Gripp, I was quite impressed with him. One day, half-kidding, I asked him, "How would you like to get into the Lord's work, Mark?"

"You don't know it, Barry, but I've resigned from GMU, and am waiting for the Lord to lead me to the next place he'd have me serve."

"What?" That was phenomenal. A man with Gripp's experience waiting for an open door! He and his wife, Rose, had served a term in Africa before he came back to direct the Canadian office of his organization. He'd traveled extensively within Canada and was perfect for the job of crusade director. By August of 1971 they were moved to London and ready for work. All we needed was an associate evangelist to take some of the meetings I had to turn down.

Before I would OK any preacher to be my associate, I really had to check him out. No ordinary, average speaker would do. From a number of sources the name Alf Rees was brought to me, and I got nothing but the highest recommendations. He was a former missionary to India and was currently pastoring the Banfield Memorial Church in Toronto. After much prayer I felt totally convinced he was my man, so I phoned him and asked if he would like to be my associate evangelist.

"But, Barry," he laughed, "I haven't met you. We've never

talked before. You've never even heard me preach."

To make a long story short, I talked to him long enough to get him to agree to hold a crusade in Hanover, Ontario. I had my associate.

Since the Lord was blessing our team so much, I figured that must be a pretty good indication that I had overcome any bitterness I had felt toward Blackwood. The Lord must have forgiven me for any wrong feelings I had held. With the world looking rosy, I set off for a crusade in Sarnia, Ontario.

On Friday evening Herb came up to me as the service was about to begin and whispered, "Jim Blackwood's in the meeting tonight."

I took a deep breath, then looked over the crowd until I spotted a familiar pudgy, boyish-looking face. I turned to Harvey and whispered the news. Then I added, "Why don't you slip down at the time of prayer and ask him if he will come to the platform at the close and give the benediction." Harv grinned and gave me a thumbs-up sign.

I preached with great ease of spirit, there was an excellent response, and then Jim came and led us in prayer. When he had closed I folded my book and went over and grabbed his hand. I couldn't help but think of the scores of times he had been on the platform with me before. "Great to have you come, man!" I said. And I meant it.

"Glad to be here," he responded, and we proceeded to talk about the new mission organization he was now heading. The old *esprit de corps* we used to have was missing. I guess the scars will always be there, but the wounds were no longer festering.

Shortly after that the world opened up for me, quite literally. The first invitation came from Victor Manogarom, the head of India Youth for Christ, asking me for a series of crusades. To set this up, and make sure the team's time was well spent, Herb Bock spent months and months corresponding with YFC in India and planned a trip himself to iron out all the kinks.

There was no way we could get along without Herb in the office for that long, so we were faced with the necessity of hiring yet another man. Bock is a very methodical, plodding type workhorse, while I'm more like a high-spirited colt who needs a bit in his mouth to keep him from going off in all directions at once. We were a great team and complemented each other beautifully.

With all the personnel changes we'd experienced through the years, I'd learned to keep a few possibilities in the back of my mind. For that reason, when Schroeder came up with some wild idea about going into politics, it didn't take long to get Steve Boalt to take over for him. The thought of Harv being elected to the Provincial House of British Columbia was so far out, I figured after the election he'd be back looking for a job. But he won! Handily.

British Columbia was still represented in the organization, however, for Jim Wilson had come into it by that time. I'd first met the Scottish immigrant with the delightful brogue in a crusade in Courtney, B. C., when some preacher brought him back after the meeting to introduce him. As we shook hands, the Lord seemed to whisper, "That's your man." So I asked him to have lunch with me the next day.

During the meal he mentioned that my message had been "like a breath of Scottish air. Biblical, and very authoritative." Now, any man who is such a connoisseur of good preaching is my kind of guy. He asked how they could have a crusade in Campbell River where he lived, just north of there. I gave my standard reply, "Invite me." The next day he was back with a letter of invitation signed by fifteen Christians from the town. He served as local chairman of the crusade a year later.

By the time Herb had to leave for India he had Wilson trained to take over some of his responsibilities. Mark left on a trip about then, too, but without my blessings. My son had tried to convince me that it was a great honor to be asked to tour with Youth For Christ's "Power and Light Company," but all I could see was that he would be missing a year of school. At eighteen he felt mature enough to make his own decisions, so off he went to perform in over 700 high schools across the Dominion.

The last crusade before India was held in Anamoose in

the northwestern corner of North Dakota. Late that Friday night the call I'd been dreading for eleven and one half years came.

"Your dad has slipped into a coma," Audrey told me. "His veins have collapsed and they've taken out the artificial feeding. They told me to call you."

Frantically I started checking transportation out of there. The nearest airport was Minot, and that isn't exactly JFK. The best I could do, by missing the closing meetings of the crusade, was to gain five hours over my scheduled departure time. I was haunted by Audrey's words, "If you want to see him alive, you should try to come home." Yet I knew he was in a coma, and probably wouldn't even know that I was there.

Ultimately I decided to stay, and prayed that he would live until I could get home. With a heavy heart and divided attention, I preached the last two sermons, and praise the Lord, he blessed anyway. We had excellent response, and I felt certain that Dad would have approved of my decision.

Butch met me at the airport and reported Dad's condition had remained unchanged. We hurried to the hospital and I tiptoed into his room. He was propped up in bed, his deep breathing audible throughout the room. With each raspy breath I thought I heard the final death rattle in his throat. I went over to the bed and put my arm across the pillow by his head and called to him loudly, "Dad! It's Barry. I'm home."

His breathing changed. I didn't know if I'd been so loud I'd scared him, or if he could really hear me or what. "Dad," I tried again, "I'm home. Dad, I know you were praying. Over one hundred people came to Christ." And he began to sob. While still in the coma!

I looked up at the nurse who was standing there watching, and she nodded encouragingly.

"Isn't that great, Dad? I just got off the plane, and I came right over to give you the report, because I knew you would be anxious and interested. I'm going home now to change my clothes, and then I'll be back to see you. Maybe you'll be feeling more rested then."

He started the deep breathing again, and I turned to the

nurse and asked, "Do you think he understood?"

"Yes. I think, from his reaction, that he understood."

I'll never forget that experience. Here my dad was at the very brink of Jordan, and he was rejoicing over the salvation of lost souls. He'd prayed while I preached. That was the way our partnership worked.

When I returned the nurse reported that his feet were cold, and she felt he was beginning to slip away. "I think he was just waiting for you to get home." Mom and Sis and I stood there together and watched him go.

Shortly after, there was a farewell rally at Wortley Church that I think would have pleased Dad immensely. Since so many people in the church were supporting our venture into India, the church gave us a special send-off. Roy Morden was at the organ, Steve Boalt sang a couple of solos, and I preached a missionary challenge.

The next morning Morden, Boalt, and I left for Scotland on our way to India. We enjoyed our time there, but when we arrived in Bombay the three of us went into culture shock. None of us had ever been in a so-called third world country before, and just the taxi ride from the airport to our hotel was traumatic. The beggars, the cardboard shacks, sacred animals, and masses of people who clogged the roads left the three of us wondering, "What in the world are we doing here?"

Before our nine weeks were over we had lived in rooms with bugs crawling up the walls, had services with monkeys shrieking in the trees, had cows wandering around in the outdoor services, and preached to 72,000 people. We were appalled by the sight of thousands sleeping in the streets, until we went to Dacca in the new nation of Bangladesh and saw them picking up the dead bodies each morning.

Boalt was plagued by sinus trouble and both he and Roy came down with dysentery, which I was determined I would not get. The heat, the schedule, and the emotional impact of all we saw took a toll on us and we were really beat after a couple months of that routine. Yet we saw nearly 2,000 people make public decisions for Christ, and that kept us going.

On our trip home we flew Thai International out of India,

Tim and Nancy.

Kerry and Paul with their three boys.

Mark and Susan.

Audrey and me in 1976.

and they gave us royal treatment just when we were desperately in need of some pampering. The trip gave us an enlarged view of the world and kindled in my heart a love for the people around the globe that I'd never had before. When at last I reached Ontario, my family was waiting for me. And Kerry Jane was flashing a diamond ring.

As never before I was aware of the dichotomy of my life. My home, my family—my world was so different from the life I'd been living on the other side of the globe. The burden of India and the Orient was still heavy on my heart, and yet I rejoiced with Kerry and Paul as they looked forward to a future together. Audrey and Kerry Jane began a flurry of preparations for the summer wedding, while I went off to my next crusade in Fredericton, New Brunswick. For years I'd felt a little guilty about leaving Butch alone with the kids so much. Now that they were growing up, I envied her a bit, for she had such a special relationship with each of them. Perhaps that's part of her reward for all the double-duty parenting she has had to do.

When the board met that spring they came to two definite decisions: we would never go overseas for such an extended time again, and in the future we would travel with a director to handle details and accommodations. The overseas invitations were coming in regularly, and it seemed the Lord was indeed making us an international organization. Another book could be written about the experiences we've had overseas, but perhaps I could share just a few of the highlights.

Three things stand out about Korea. One is the sound of the singing drifting into the windows of our hotel rooms from the predawn prayer meetings held a mile and a half away at the park. The Korean Christians could teach us a good deal about prayer. The sight of the final meeting when 62,000 people came and sat on little mats to hear me preach is etched in my mind. Then there is the vision of my lovely wife, decked out in full Oriental dress, being presented to the people. It had been a delightful surprise for me when a friend made it possible for her to travel with me to Korea, but when she tiptoed shyly out on that platform, gave a sweet smile, and bowed, she charmed the whole audience.

The next year we were in Italy, Ireland, India, Scotland, and Korea. That was also the year that Mark entered Houghton College and made the Dean's list. I always knew he could do it if he tried. This was partly due, I felt, to the influence of a young lady named Susan Hawke. Susan was a new Christian with a determined dedication who also encouraged Mark in his music and song writing.

I don't want to give the impression that when all the overseas crusades opened up, we forgot our first commitment to Canada and the small out-of-the-way places. That year we held crusades with full teams in sixteen towns with populations of less than 3,000: spots like Tofield, Alberta; Boissevain, Manitoba; Yellowknife, Northwest Territories; and Metlakatla, Alaska.

One evening that year, for some reason I had an off night and I went to watch Tim play volleyball. It was the first time I'd ever seen Tim play any sport. He played his heart out that night, and it made me realize how much I'd missed. Tim had always been such a good-natured kid, and so pleasant to have around, that it was easy to take him for granted. A few nights later when I was going over my schedule for the coming months, I called him over. "How would you like to go to Europe with me as a sort of graduation present?"

A wide grin ignited his face. "Wow! Yeah!"

"Well, then, I'll start working on the financing." It wound up that Tim paid his plane fare over, and I took care of the rest.

The team was booked for a crusade just outside of Belfast, North Ireland, that spring and Tim was to fly over and join me for the final meetings. Then we would tour Europe, stopping to visit with missionary friends on the continent. Well, when I deplaned in Belfast, I began having second thoughts about Tim coming in there alone. The airport looked like an old World War II movie with soldiers, holding rifles, posted up and down the corridors. Stepping outside, I saw military vehicles and armored cars all around.

We drove to Ballynahinch, fourteen miles from Belfast, where a huge 2,400-seat tent had been erected. Jim Wilson was serving as crusade director and he had everything well organized. Roy Morden was with me again on this trip, and he was to direct the choir as well as play the organ. As guest soloist we had Ed Lyman. And the Ulster folks seemed enthralled at a non-Irish tenor with such a magnificent voice. The crowds were excellent and we had responses to the invitation each night.

Since Tim's plane was due just a couple of hours before the services, Wilson thought it would be best to have someone not needed on the platform to meet him, just in case the plane might be late. He sent a minister with a crusade poster of me, so Tim would recognize him as a friend. In a touchy situation like North Ireland, you have to be careful.

It got later and later, and no Tim. It was growing dark as we began the services. We had gone through all the preliminaries, and Ed was just about to sing the final solo before the message when Wilson led a fuzzy-headed, sleepy-looking eighteen-year-old up on the platform. Tim plopped down beside me, needing a shave and wearing disheveled-looking corduroys. But he looked good to me. I introduced my son to the crowd, and he seemed embarrassed but pleased at the applause he was given.

The next night, after he had cleaned up, I had him read the Bible passage before the prayer time. I was very proud of him, and pleased that he could have part in my ministry and see a bit of what God was doing around the world.

For the final meeting 3,000 people tried to fit under the tent. There was a real air of excitement, of anticipation, as the meeting began. Then, right in the middle of my sermon, a young man got up and began making his way to the platform.

That might not get much of a reaction in North America, but believe me, you could feel the tension in that crowd. They had seen so many senseless tragedies, that the thought of a "living bomb" coming to blow up himself, the evangelist, and hundreds of Protestants came to many minds. People moved to the edges of their seats, ready to dive for cover.

"Why have you come, young man?" I asked with a bit of a catch in my throat.

"I want to receive Christ," he replied with great conviction.

One of the men led him to the nearby counseling tent, and after the services I was introduced to him. A member of the British Army, he had just returned from border patrol when some friends influenced him to come to the services. He became one of a host of conversions in that crusade.

While Tim and I were driving through ten countries in northern Europe following the crusade, I was delighted to discover that he shared my lifelong interest in history. We stopped at Dunkirk, Bastogne, and Waterloo, visiting the scenes of famous battles. The spot most impressive to us as Canadians was the memorial on Vimy Ridge commemorating the 3,500 Canadians who had given their lives taking the ridge during World War I. The huge Canadian flag that flies over the site, the free tour extended to Canadian citizens, and the fact that I shared the experience with my son, made this a special day for me.

Then it was home for Mark and Susan's wedding. Mark hadn't earned his degree yet, because of the year touring. But Susan was going to work and help him finish. Then he was planning on going into full-time Christian service either with his music, or as an educational director. They seemed extremely level-headed and committed to each other. An excellent match.

About that time I needed to strike up a match myself. Steve Boalt was going to leave the team, and I wanted to get a man who would stick with me. All I wanted was an outstanding soloist, who was also an experienced choir director, and who had the personality and wit to emcee the program. Schroeder did it all back in the good old days. It seemed there should be someone who could fill all those roles.

My old buddy, Ken Carter, came with me as guest soloist for the Regina crusade, and I talked to him about my problem. Carter had been serving as music director in his home church in Memphis since leaving me, and had picked up just the experience he needed to qualify him on all counts. So I took him for another lunch and explained what I needed. "Are you interested? I've got to have someone who can do it all and be my buddy, too."

"Well, I've been doing it all for the past four years. I've got ten choirs, a weekly TV program, four radio programs, plus schools of music, banquets, and a tape ministry. I have less time with my family now than I'd have being on the road. Besides, I'm your friend."

"So you are interested?"

"I'll have to talk with Sherry."

Carter signed on again in September of 1976.

The first overseas crusade that Carter participated in was also one of our most exciting. The Philippines. The month of February was devoted to a saturation-type evangelism as the whole staff ministered in nine different cities. There were daily sessions for pastors attended by 500 ministers from all over the islands.

The night the 600-voice choir sang Handel's "Hallelujah Chorus" the 7,500 people in the audience sat spellbound. A noted musician was so impressed by Carter's voice that Ken was extended an invitation to sing in a series of concerts sponsored by the First Lady, Madame Marcos. Most important, there were thousands of decisions registered.

Later I heard from a missionary who had heard the broadcast of the concluding service of the Greater Manila Crusade in Peking, China. He had dialed the Far East Broadcasting Network that Sunday afternoon and had heard the message clearly. In the sermon I had mentioned my concern for the audience spread across Southeast Asia, and the report that the message had been heard behind the Bamboo Curtain was thrilling news.

I needed that encouragement about then, because we were soon to embark on a really dangerous mission. A crusade in my hometown. The Scriptures have something to say about a prophet in his own territory, and I'll have to admit that I was a bit uptight about the prospect of falling flat on my face in front of the hometown folks, but God was faithful. The concluding services were held at the Western Fair Grounds with 5,000 in attendance. We had hundreds of inquirers who responded to the Act of Witness.

A thrill of another kind came of June 15, when Paul

Jason Whitelaw was born, making us grandparents. We got to see him the day they brought him home. For both Audrey and me it was love at first sight. A perfect, precious, healthy doll.

A couple of months later we had our first excursion into South Africa. Our first meeting was in Dundee, and that Sunday morning we held services in a neutral building and all the churches were closed. We had a cross-cultural, cross-denominational, cross-racial meeting, conducted by the local ministers, and we celebrated communion. It was the first time such a service was held in the history of the area, and it was beautiful. It was a remarkable demonstration that in spite of the many deep problems in South Africa, God is still working. The question we were asked most often was, "When will you be back?"

That question is indicative of the doors that have opened over the world. Since Schroeder made that prediction we have maintained a 20 percent annual increase in all phases of the ministry. We've doubled the size of our staff since then. The Lord even demonstrated his sense of humor when Kerry Jane was to produce our second grandchild, and it turned out to be identical twins: David Nelson and Jonathan Bradley.

One new member of the team I must mention is our minister of youth, Mark Moore. Despite my fear of cries of nepotism, the Board hired Mark when he proved the best man we could find for the job. Mark had been in two youth groups, served as a minister of youth in a Toronto church, and had earned his B.A. from Houghton College. His year of touring with Power and Light was just the experience needed to make him the ideal candidate for the job.

Another platform man creates a need for more backup personnel. Success is our biggest problem, for we are continually in need of new personnel, time to fill the invitations that come our way, and resources to pay the freight. It's exciting to be part of a work that remains fresh and growing and exciting after twenty-plus years. There is no doubt in my mind that God has blessed our efforts and will continue to do so.

At the marriage of Tim to Nancy Marshall, his blessings

on my family were much in evidence also. Tim and Nancy had both grown up at Wortley Church and had known each other all their lives, since our families had been close friends. It seemed particularly fitting that all three of our children had been married in the same church where Audrey and I were united in matrimony.

As the wedding ceremony began, I looked over at Butch and she gave me a big grin. Kerry Jane was beaming almost as maternally, for she had been Tim's baby-sitter when she was in her teens. I was really pleased with Kerry. Her three young sons kept her tied down, yet she and Paul made time to be active in their church in Toronto. Her testimony for the Lord was strong and clear.

Mark and Susan got up to sing a wedding song that Mark had written for the occasion, and I praised God for this. My relationship with Mark had improved a great deal since I had come to realize he was his own man. He had proven himself a valuable asset to our team, and his dedication to Christ was an inspiration. I felt very proud of him.

And Tim. Standing there with his face aglow, watching his lovely young bride coming down the aisle toward him. There had never been any doubt about his relationship to Christ since the time he came forward in one of my crusades to make a public declaration of his faith. Now he and Nancy would be serving the Lord together in Regina, Saskatchewan, where he had accepted the position of director of athletics at the Canadian Bible College.

Standing there, watching my three children who had turned into such fine young adults, I felt very grateful for each of them.

And you're not in debt either. The impact of that thought was immediate. I recalled the pact I had made with the Lord years before when I first committed myself to full-time service. I had asked the Lord to keep my children in his love, and to keep me out of debt. He has fulfilled that covenant! I can say with Joshua of old that not one thing has failed of all the good things which the Lord my God promised concerning me; all have come to pass for me; not one has failed.